WHEN THEY APPEARED

Falcon Lake 1967:
The inside story of a close encounter

Stan Michalak & Chris Rutkowski

Plus the original story
My Encounter With The UFO
by
Stephen Michalak

www.augustnightbooks.com

For Maria and Stefan Michalak

TABLE OF CONTENTS

PART 1

Introduction

By Chris Rutkowski

INTRODUCTION

In June, 1947, a businessman named Kenneth Arnold was piloting a small plane near Mt. Rainer in the state of Washington in the USA. He was at about 9,000 feet over the mountains when he saw nine flying objects that he could not identify.

This was the first official report of flying saucers and is considered the beginning of the modern UFO phenomenon. Since then, literally hundreds of thousands of people around the world have reported seeing strange unidentified flying objects.

Arnold's sighting made international news headlines, and in the weeks following his experience, many sightings of saucer-like craft were reported across North America. Manitoba, like any location on the continent, was not spared the onslaught of UFOs in its skies.

The oldest account of an odd object over Manitoba took place in the fall of 1792. Explorers David Thompson and Andrew Davy were camped on the shore of Landing Lake, near what is now Thicket Portage. In Thompson's diary, he recorded that one night he and his companion were surprised by the appearance of a brilliant "meteor of globular form... larger than the Moon." This object seemed to move directly towards them, descended slightly, and "when within

3

three hundred yards of us, it struck the River ice with a sound like a mass of jelly, was dashed in innumerable luminous pieces and instantly expired." Thompson noted that the next morning, when they went to see the hole it should have made in the ice, they could not find any sign of the object's apparent impact on the Earth.

I have collected more than 2,000 sightings of unidentified flying objects over Manitoba reported since that time. These reports include observations by people from all walks of life: from farmers, pilots, campers and police. There are reports noted in newspapers, mailed to civilian investigators and posted to Facebook groups. Cases have been obtained from private records, RCMP files, Canadian Forces documents and the National Archives in Ottawa.

For example, on July 15, 1947, at about 3:15 a.m., Winnipeg telegraph operator Homer Clinton had just returned home from his shift when he heard a "noisy disturbance" in his back yard. He and his wife and son ran out to watch a "whatzit" in the northwest sky near the Big Dipper. The object was starlike in appearance, but it moved on a zig-zag course and would periodically "flop over" as it flew. The three witnesses observed the noisy object for about 15 minutes before it gained altitude and was lost to sight.

In Canada, official interest in reports of such unusual flying craft led to government-sponsored studies of UFOs: *Project Second Storey* and *Project Magnet*. Both were relatively short-lived and were associated with a controversial electronics specialist named Wilbert B. Smith. During the course of his work in the Department of National Defence, Smith became convinced that UFOs represented alien contact, though his view was not shared by his superiors. However, Smith claimed he had been privy to top level meetings with both Canadian and American military personnel, and he was told at these meetings that flying saucers were considered to be of major concern to the American military. Later in his career, Smith claimed to actually have been in contact with the aliens, who had begun preliminary negotiations for an official landing at a Canadian military base.

According to the files of *Project Second Storey*, on July 29, 1952, at about 11:00 p.m., a witness at MacDonald Airport north of Winnipeg watched an orange, oblong, stationary object in the south-southwest sky for about two minutes. The aerial craft was about 15 degrees above the horizon and was calculated to be about six miles away from the airfield. As the witness watched, the craft seemed to change into a group of smaller, round lights, then they disappeared altogether.

The American presence in Manitoba during the Cold War was quite significant. The 916th Base near Beausejour at Milner Ridge was a major radar facility for monitoring objects flying south towards the United States. A former duty officer in the radar operations building there claimed that in the fall of 1956, he detected a strange object moving south over Eastern Manitoba. It was a strong return, indicative of a solid object such as an aircraft, and about 175 miles northeast of Milner Ridge. He was surprised when the second trace on the radarscope showed it had moved a great distance from the first plot.

In order to confirm the return, he checked the height and range indicator and calculated the object's altitude to be 75,000 feet. When he spotted the object again, the equipment suggested that its speed was between 6,000 and 7,500 knots — faster than any known aircraft at the time. He explained: "If I had not confirmed its location on the two independent systems, I would have just passed it off as a malfunction."

He tracked the object for about ten minutes as it flew a straight course with slight changes in direction, but always at the same altitude. The nearest it came to the base was around MacArthur Falls. He reported it to the chief controller, who labelled it a malfunction. However, the radar officer was called into the controller's office the next day and instructed never to tell anyone what he had seen.

And then, in 1967, only twenty years after Arnold's watershed sighting, Stefan Michalak decided to travel to Falcon Lake for a weekend of amateur prospecting. His story of encountering and getting physically injured by a strange, saucer-shaped vehicle has been recounted numerous times in print and in media, including several re-creations on popular UFO-themed TV shows. He was blasted by hot gas as the craft departed, setting fire to his clothes as well as nearby forest vegetation. He was physically ill and had to be taken to a hospital where doctors treated his burns, but he continued to suffer effects of his encounter and took months to recuperate. This was perhaps too much of a "close encounter" with a UFO.

Michalak was interrogated by the RCAF and RCMP. He led officials to the area, where the Department of Health and Welfare found such high levels of radiation that they considered cordoning off the area out of a concern for public safety.

Michalak spent a great deal of his own money travelling to the Mayo Clinic, as it was not covered by Medicare. The physicians there could find no obvious explanation for his injuries, and a psychiatrist concluded he was not the type of person who would make up a bizarre tale. If it was a hoax, it is the most contrived on record, involving radiation, contaminated soil, medical examinations and a flurry of investigations by government officials at many levels. What's more, Access to Information requests and perusal of records in the National Archives of Canada have uncovered as many as one hundred official documents about the military and government investigations. Civilian records and reports number in the hundreds as well, helping to make the Falcon Lake case one of the best-documented on record, easily surpassing some of the classic and well-known UFO cases such as Roswell and Shag Harbour.

But in addition to the documents and physical evidence, there is another aspect of Michalak's experience that is rarely mentioned. That is the enormous impact his experience had on his family, who had to endure the appearance on their doorstep of a multitude of media, military and civilian investigators, and curiosity-seekers. Although Michalak's experience had been physically painful, the discomfort and disruption created as fallout from the incident resulted in emotional and mental trauma to all family members for many following years.

Stan Michalak was only nine years old when his father had the experience at Falcon Lake. But he remembers clearly how his life changed dramatically during the weeks and years after the event. He believes it is important to share with the public the "other side" of the story that most people never get to know: how a significant UFO case affects not only the primary witness, but also those who are intimately involved with the ensuing investigations and attempts to explain what had occurred.

When They Appeared tries to tell the entire story of Michalak's experience. This book starts with Stefan Michalak himself telling his story in his own words, in a faithful reprint of the privately-published booklet that has been out of print since 1968. Then, Michalak's son Stan describes how his father's experience affected his own life and that of his mother and siblings. I describe in detail how the official and civilian investigations took place, and the conclusions reached by the various players. I later offer my own personal view of my involvement in the Michalak case as a science writer and investigator of unusual events. A number of official documents and images are presented that indicate how various agencies viewed Michalak's experience. Included are transcripts of some interrogations by investigators, to give a more complete picture of what transpired and a peek into the minds of some of those involved.

In the report of the United States government-sponsored UFO project, the *Condon Report*, Michalak's experience was described as "unknown," implying there was no explanation for his experience. Its concluding remarks were impressive: "If (the case) were physically real, it would show the existence of alien flying vehicles in our environment."

Fifty years after it happened, it is likely that many questions about the case may never be resolved. It is an interesting chapter in Canadian history, showing the interaction between officialdom and a witness to something remarkable and terrifying in the wilderness of Manitoba. When they appeared, visitors and investigators changed the lives of the Michalaks forever.

Chris Rutkowski
March, 2017

Authors' Note: Stefan Michalak's first name was often anglicized to Stephen, Steven or Steve. We have stayed faithful to his original Polish given name, Stefan, where possible but have retained the various forms used in his book, official documents and interviews.

PART 2

My Encounter With The UFO

By Stephen Michalak

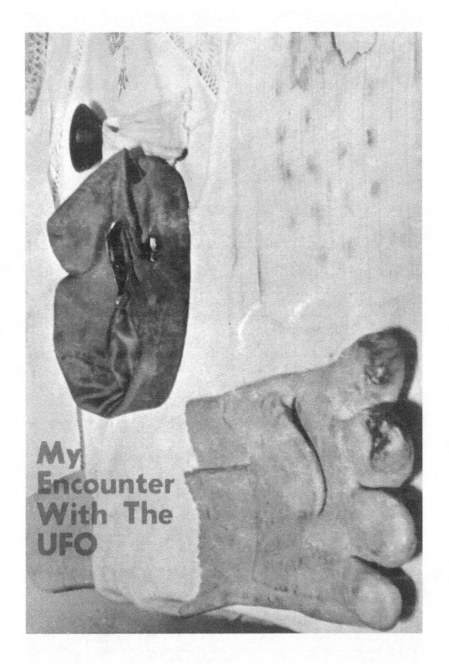

A non-colour scan of the original cover of *My Encounter With The UFO*.

My Encounter With The UFO

By Stephen Michalak
From Author's manuscript in Polish re-told by Paul Pihichyn

Published by
OSNOVA PUBLICATIONS
Winnipeg, Man. 1967 Canada

Authors' Note: We have retained Stefan Michalak's manuscript as it was published in 1967, including any grammatical errors that were missed at that time, in order to preserve its authenticity.

FOREWORD

When I was approached by Stephen Michalak to write the English version of his story, I was sceptical. I did not believe in the existence of extra-terrestrial life, and the phenomena called UFOs.

After helping with the English translation of the original Polish manuscript by Mr. Michalak I began to wonder if I had been wrong. I wondered if perhaps there could have been a landing at Falcon Lake on May 20, 1967.

But I still wasn't convinced.

I talked to several people mentioned in the book. I read accounts of the sighting which appeared in the press and in magazines. And after weighing all the facts, I felt sure that Stephen Michalak did indeed witness the landing of an alien craft.

A word on the original text. Mr. Michalak has made notes on his observations, and events that followed. Recently he compiled these into chronological account of what happened in Polish, his native language. His only purpose in doing so was to inform the public of this uncanny occurrence and the strange effects it had upon him.

Through talking with him, I have found that he is not a man who would exaggerate or distort or fabricate such a tale. The events described in this book are true.

It is interesting to note that the Canadian Press carried a report on November 6, 1967 saying that the Government of Canada refused to disclose any information they had discovered during investigation of the claims by Mr. Michalak.

In the words of Defence Minister Cadieux "It is not the intention of the department of national defence to make public the report of the alleged sighting."

If the investigation had shown that the "alleged sighting" was pure fabrication, is it not conceivable that the government would have made it known, and cleared up any doubts or fears the public may have. But instead, the federal government chose to remain silent. This can mean only two things: either they have definite proof, unknown to Mr. Michalak and myself, or they know something extraordinary happened but cannot or dare not explain it.

It is up to you, the reader, to make your own decision.

Paul Pihichyn

INTRODUCTION

My name is Stephen Michalak. I was born 51 years ago in Poland. After the turbulent years of the Second World War that started in my homeland, and due to the events that followed, I was forced to leave my country and go abroad.

In 1949 I came to Canada, and some years later, settled in Winnipeg, Manitoba. I live with my wife, two sons and a daughter in a modest home. I have a steady income from my job as a mechanic at the Inland Cement Company. Two of my children attend the University of Manitoba. We live a happy, satisfied life of average Canadians, fully enjoying all the blessings this country is offering us.

Up until the time and the events I am about to describe I had no special interests in "flying saucers" and other strange phenomena one hears about time and again. I heard and read about them, but they meant to me about as much as the Loch Ness monster. Maybe they are real, maybe not, but I had never been seriously concerned about them.

Not until May 20, 1967, when I, perhaps as nobody else – or at least very few – came in such a close contact with one of those strange objects commonly called UFOs.

How it all began, how I happened to be in the vicinity of the actual landing of the UFO and my strange encounter with it – will be explained herein.

I am what one may call an amateur prospector. For many years, mostly early in the spring, this being the most favourable time for prospecting in the wooded and rocky terrain of eastern Manitoba, I go and look for minerals. I have even made a few claims.

When the spring of 1967 came I decided to spend the first long weekend in the Whiteshell area – lying about 80 miles east of Winnipeg.

So, early in the evening on Friday, May 19, I took the Greyhound bus to Falcon Lake and settled down for the night in a motel with the idea of getting up early in the morning and "trying my luck," as I said to myself.

Little did I know then what kind of "luck" I was to find the next day.

THE LANDING

It was 5.30 a.m. when I left the motel and started out on my geologic trek. I took with me a hammer, a map, a compass, paper and pencil and a little food to see me through the day, wearing a light jacket against the morning chill.

The day was bright, sunny – not a cloud in the sky. It seemed like just another ordinary day, but events which were to take place within the next six hours were to change my entire life more than anyone could ever imagine. I will never forget May 20, 1967.

Crossing the Trans-Canada Highway from the motel on the south side, I made my way into the bush and the pine forest on the north side. After travelling some distance I got out my map and compass and orientated myself.

By nine o'clock I had found an area that particularly fascinated me because of the rock formation near a bog along a stream flowing in the southward direction. I was searching for some special specimens that I had found on my earlier expedition.

My approach had startled a flock of geese, but before long they became accustomed to my presence, quieted down and went about their business.

At 11 o'clock I began to feel the effects of the breakfast I did not eat that morning. I sat down and took out the lunch I

15

had brought with me. Following a simple meal of smoked sausage, cheese and bread, an apple and two oranges washed down with a couple of cups of coffee, and after a short rest, I returned to the quartz vein I was examining. It was 12:15, the sun was high in the sky and a few clouds were gathering in the west.

While chipping at the quartz I was startled by the most uncanny cackle of the geese that were still in the area. Something had obviously frightened them far more than my presence earlier in the morning when they gave out a mild protest.

Then I saw them. Two cigar-shaped objects with humps on them about halfway down from the sky. They appeared to be descending and glowing with an intense scarlet glare. As these "objects" came closer to the earth they became more oval-shaped.

They came down at the same speed keeping a constant distance between them, appearing to be as one inseparable unit, yet each one completely separate from the other.

Suddenly the farthest of the two objects – farthest from my point of vision – stopped dead in the air while its companion slipped down closer and closer to the ground and landed squarely on the flat top of a rock about 160 feet away from me.

The "object" that had remained in the air hovered approximately 15 feet above me for about three minutes, then lifted skyward again.

As it ascended its colour began to change from bright red to an orange shade, then to a grey tone. Finally, when it was just about to disappear behind the gathering clouds, it again turned bright orange.

The "craft," if I may be allowed to call it a craft, had appeared and disappeared in such a short time that it was impossible to estimate the length of the time it remained visible. My astonishment at and fear of the unusual sight that I had just witnessed dulled my senses and made me lose all realization of time.

I cannot describe or estimate the speed of the ascent because I have seen nothing in the world that moved so swiftly, noiselessly, without a sound.

THE CRAFT

Then my attention was drawn back to the craft that had landed on the rock. It too was changing in colour, turning from red to grey-red to light grey and then to the colour of hot stainless steel, with a golden glow around it.

I realized that I was still kneeling on the rock with my small hammer in my hand. I was still wearing goggles which I used to protect my eyes from the rock chips.

After recovering my composure and regaining my senses to some degree I began watching the craft intently, ready to record in my mind everything that happened.

I noticed an opening near the top of the craft and a brilliant purple light pouring out of an aperture. The light was so intense that it hurt my eyes when I looked at it directly. Gripped with fear and excitement, I was unable to move from the rock. I decided to wait and watch.

Soon I became aware of wafts of warm air that seemed to come out in waves from the craft, accompanied by the pungent odour of sulphur. I heard a soft murmur, like the whirl of a tiny electric motor running very fast. I also heard a hissing sound as if the air had been sucked into the interior of the craft.

It was now that I wanted a camera more than anything else, but, of course, there is no need for one on a geologic expedition. Then I remembered the paper and pencil that I had brought with me. I made a sketch of what I saw. By now some of the initial fear had left me and I managed to gather enough courage to get closer to the craft and to investigate. I fully expected someone to get out at any moment and survey the landing site.

Because I have never seen anything like this before, I thought it may have been an American space project of some sort. I checked for the markings of the United States Air Force on the hull of the craft but found nothing.

I was most interested in the flood of lights that poured out of the upper reaches of the craft. The light, distinctly purple, also cast various other shades.

In spite of the bright mid-day sun in the sky, the light cast a purple hue on the ground and eclipsed the sunlight in the immediate area.

I was forced to continually turn my eyes away from the light which made red dots to appear before my eyes every time I looked away.

I approached the object closer, coming to within 60 feet of the glowing mass of metal. Then I heard voices. They sounded like human, although somewhat muffled by the sounds of the motor and the rush of air that was continuously coming out from somewhere inside. I was able to make out two distinct voices, one with a higher pitch than the other.

The latest discovery added to my excitement and I was sure that the craft was of an earthly origin. I came even closer and beckoned to those inside: "Okay, Yankee boys, having trouble? Come on out and we'll see what we can do about it."

There was no answer and no sign from within. I had prepared myself for some response and was taken aback when none came. I was at a loss, perplexed. I didn't know what to do next.

But then, more to encourage myself than anything else, I addressed the voices in Russian asking them if they spoke Russian. No answer. I tried again in German, Italian, French and Ukrainian. Still no answer.

Then I spoke again in English and walked closer to the craft. By now I found myself directly in front of it and decided to take a look inside. However, standing within the beam of light was too much for my eyes to bear. I was forced to turn away. Then, placing green lenses over my goggles, I stuck my head inside the opening.

The inside was a maze of lights. Direct beams running in horizontal and diagonal paths and a series of flashing lights, it seemed to me, were working in a random fashion, with no particular order or sequence.

Again I stepped back and awaited some reaction from the craft. As I did this I took note of the thickness of the walls of the craft. They were about 20 inches thick at the cross-section.

Then came the first sign of motion since the craft touched down.

Two panels slid over the opening and a third piece dropped over them from above. This completely closed off the opening in the side of the craft.

Then I noticed a small screen pattern on the side of the craft. It seemed to be some sort of ventilation system. The screen openings appeared to be about 3/16 of an inch in diameter.

I approached the craft once again and touched its side. It was hot to touch. It appeared to be made of a steel-like substance. There were no signs of welding or joints to be seen anywhere. The outer surface was highly polished and looked like coloured glass with light reflecting off it. It formed a spectrum with a sliver background as the sunlight hit the sides.

I noticed that I had burned my glove I was wearing at the time, when I touched the side of the craft.

These most recent events occurred in less time than it takes to describe them.

All of a sudden the craft tilted slightly leftward. I turned

19

and felt a scorching pain around my chest; my shirt and my undershirt were afire. A sharp beam of heat had shot from the craft. I tore off my shirt and undershirt and threw them to the ground. My chest was severely burned.

When I looked back at the ship I felt a sudden rush of air around me. The craft was rising above the treetops. It began to change colour and shape, following much the same pattern as its sister ship when it had returned to the sky. Soon the craft had disappeared, gone without a trace.

AFTERMATH

As I stood there with a thousand thoughts racing through my mind, I was unable to move or to act. I was taken aback by fear and bewilderment. It was hard to believe that these things actually happened to me.

Reason told me that it had to be some earthly thing, but evidence pointed out to something else. I recalled, as I stood gazing at the rock where only seconds ago the craft had sat, an article I once read in *Life Magazine*. It told of other civilizations on other planets, other worlds. At the time I took it with a grain of salt, believing it to be the result of someone's fertile imagination. Now I began to wonder whether there was not some foundation for it after all.

The odour, that reminded me of an odour of burning electric motor mixed with strong smell of sulphur, still hung in the air. Looking down, I noticed some dry moss burning near my discarded shirts. Automatically, I stamped out the fire with my feet. The woods were extremely dry and a fire now could possibly trap me.

Again I turned my thought to the events and scenes I had just witnessed. Walking over to the rock where I had left my bag and compass, I began to pick up my things.

When I looked at the compass, I saw the needle whirling around, completely out of control, as if some strange magnetic force had been controlling it. Seconds later it became still, working normally.

Somehow my desire for prospecting had vanished. I decided to go over to the landing site and make a thorough inspection of the place where the craft had touched down.

As I approached the site I felt nauseated and my head began to ache. The spot where the craft had come to rest looked as if it had been swept clean with a broom. There was no debris of any kind on the rock. No twigs, bits of stone – nothing. It had all been piled up in a six inches deep circular mound about 15 feet in diameter.

As I stood there examining the spot, the pain in my head became more severe. Waves of nausea increased and I broke out in a cold sweat.

I knew that something totally unnatural had happened to me and, apparently, it was having adverse effect on my physiology.

I might add that up to this time I had been as healthy as any man could expect to be. My weight was a constant 180 pounds, and I had not been sick a day in the last 25 years. The only times I went to a doctor was for the regular insurance company check-ups.

Now it was obvious that something was wrong. Very wrong. I vomited. A feeling of weakness was coming over me and I became really alarmed. I knew that I must get back to civilization as soon as possible.

I returned to the place where I was when all this happened and gathered up my equipment. Then I started walking back towards the highway and Falcon Lake.

THE ORDEAL

I had not gone far when I was forced to stop and vomit. Again and again my stomach heaved and swayed. My mouth was hot and dry. The pain in my head got worse. All the food I consumed was gone from my stomach, but I continued to vomit green bile.

The same kind of pink dots that appeared in front of my eyes when I looked at the light in the craft returned.

I came upon the brook I had passed on my way into the area. Bending down, I slopped water all over my face and head. I had to remain conscious. To stop now would be fatal.

Using the compass was impossible. I couldn't make out the direction of the needle because I was unable to see straight. Instead, I searched for some familiar landmarks. With great effort in every step I made my way in what I hoped was the right direction, praying that every step would bring me closer to safety.

I had to continue stopping every so often to vomit. The ever-worsening splitting headache added to my misery. Now I felt a burning on my chest. Red marks had appeared where the blast from the craft touched me and burnt my shirt. Some spots were as large as silver dollars. I removed my jacket because it irritated the sores when the cloth touched them. I kept on walking naked from the waist up.

Before long I was to experience another chilling fright. I saw an unfamiliar path which I had not seen before. I thought that I became lost. But, I reasoned, the path may lead me to the highway. I prayed that it would. I began to follow it and soon heard cars passing by on the road.

I was desperately in need of medical attention. Sweat ran into my eyes and I could hardly see where I was going as I stumbled along the path and finally got onto the highway.

As I stood there catching my breath I began wondering how I could ever explain the thing I had just seen and experienced. My wife and children would never believe me. And what about my neighbours and friends? It was so unearthly, so unbelievable – like an apparition. How could I defend myself, should people say I was crazy? Hundreds of thoughts flashed through and puzzled my mind. It was impossible to decide there and then what to do. I knew I must get help fast. That was my concern at the moment.

I knew there was an RCMP detachment at Falcon Lake. There, I hoped, I could at least get some medical aid and care. Besides, it was my duty to report to the authorities what I had witnessed.

I walked out onto the highway and discovered that I was about a mile west of the point where I had entered the woods that morning. I directed my steps eastward, hardly able to move my feet. I made some small progress growing weaker with every step.

My heartbeat quickened when I saw an RCMP car approaching. I raised and waved my hand frantically, but the car passed by without stopping. I was amazed at their apparent indifference to my signalling.

The only thing to do was to continue walking. I made very slow progress; my stomach was still churning and my head was pounding like a drum. My only thought was to get to Falcon Lake as soon as possible.

The odour of "burning electric motor" and sulphur lingered about me, constantly bringing back to my mind the things I had seen.

As I staggered along the roadside I heard a voice calling me. Turning, I saw an RCMP constable. Briefly I gave him an account of what had happened – warning him not to come to close to me because I feared the possibility of spreading radiation. I asked about medical aid. "Sorry, but I have duties to perform here," he said. I stared at him, unbelieving what I had just heard. He, apparently, did not believe a word I told him. Otherwise he would have acted differently.

The constable left me with my sickness and disappointment. Yet I thought: every human being, no matter how small or how great, has at one time or another found within himself great ambition to accomplish what seems to be impossible. I knew that for me such a time had come now.

At long last I was within the sight of my motel at Falcon Lake. My journey took every ounce of strength I had left in me. By the time I reached the motel I was totally exhausted. I did not go inside the motel for fear of contaminating people around me. I remained outside in the woods nearby.

I felt detached from the rest of the world. All my strength was gone and the pain in my head reached the limits of human endurance. My eyes felt as if they were bulging out from my head, and the pain was unbearable when I turned my head to look around.

With every breath, the stench of sulphur returned. I took a deep breath trying to rid myself of the foul smell and the nausea it brought about, but it didn't help. The odour seemed to come from within me and I could not escape it.

I was afraid that I had ruined my health and visualized the resulting hell should I become disabled. To the exclusion of everything else my mind centred upon the possible consequences flowing out of what had just happened. The pains continued and became more severe than ever.

By four o'clock that afternoon I could stand it no longer. I got out and went to the motel's restaurant, asking a waitress if a doctor was available. She said that the resident physician would not arrive until July and that the nearest doctor was in Kenora, Ontario, 45 miles east of Falcon Lake.

With this latest setback I had no alternative but to go to my room and rest. There had to be some way of getting medical aid and attention.

I thought of the press. Things that happened to me were definitely news, if nothing else. So I contacted the *Winnipeg Tribune* – only to find that I had again drawn a blank. It was Saturday afternoon and there was no one in the office who could have helped me.

Large and small pink spots appeared on my chest as the result of burns I received from the heat of the craft. I did not want to alarm my wife, or cause panic in the family. I phoned her as a last resort, telling her that I had been in an accident and that I had suffered some burns to my chest. We arranged to have my son Mark meet me at the bus depot in Winnipeg later that evening. Now at least I seemed to be getting a little closer to safety.

Returning to my room, I packed and checked out – only to find that I had four hours to wait for the bus! I felt sick, very sick, and all cold, and hot, and cold again. I put on a sweater and an overcoat, but the chills kept recurring.

I left for the bus stop long before the bus was due to arrive. Not wanting to mix with people because of the possibility of my spreading radiation, I waited in the background.

As I sat on a tree stump on the boulevard, suffering pain and the stench and the coloured spots all around me, I began to reflect upon my life. Flashing through my mind were horrors of the war with its total disregard of human life, its valour and its cowardice. I recalled instances when I had closer brushes with death and survived. This thought comforted me and I felt that somehow I'll pull through my present harrowing experience.

After what seemed an eternity, the bus arrived. I boarded it and gave my ticket to the driver. He looked at me the way one looks at a drunk. I could almost feel what went on in his mind, but he had no idea how utterly wrong he was.

I moved to the rear of the bus, hoping to separate myself

from the other passengers by the greatest possible distance. I wanted no contact with people now. It was a relief to know that I would be home soon.

My eldest son, Mark, met me at the Winnipeg bus depot at 10:15 that evening and took me directly to the Misericordia Hospital.

THE SCRUTINY

A doctor examined the burns on my chest and gave me a sedative. He asked me how I got burnt. Excuses flashed through my mind, and I told him that I had been hit by exhaust coming out of an aeroplane.

At this point I must explain the reason for contradicting the recent events, and avoid confusing the reader. The doctor who treated me was of Chinese origin and, while being a fine and competent physician, I am sure, he was not too well versed in the English language... and neither am I. I felt that there could be some misunderstanding and what's more: I did not feel up to relating the whole story just then. I was thinking how to get home as soon as possible, without any delay that my true revelation might have caused. Besides, the pain I was suffering was too much for me to go through it all again.

My son took me home. After a bath I took a sedative and went to bed – hoping that morning will bring a brighter day.

The following day proved to be no better. The pain was just as bad, the awful stench still lingered in my lungs and the dots still danced in front of my eyes. The vomiting had stopped. It was quite a relief. Strangely, I was not hungry. I realized that I had not eaten since I had seen the craft in the woods the day before.

Efforts to drink a little tea proved useless. No sooner had

I swallowed it when I began to vomit again.

I weighed myself and found that I had lost six pounds since yesterday – more cause for concern.

The throbbing pain in my head persisted no matter how I sat, turned or laid down. Only the loyal support and understanding of my family sustained my strength and lifted my spirit.

In the evening Miss Heather Chisvin, *Winnipeg Tribune* reporter, together with a photographer came to the house. I didn't realize, as I recounted the events of the previous day, that this was a beginning of long series of questions and harassment by the press, radio, television, the air force and various authorities.

I did not sleep that night, nevertheless I felt a little better the next morning. I had never taken any medicines before, but now I decided to try some 292s. I took two of them, but they did not seem to do much good.

My wife called our family doctor, Dr. R.D. Oatway. I repeated to him the whole story. He looked at me with what one may call a professional discretion and told me to eat some sugar and salt. He also prescribed some sea-sickness tablets, and more 292s.

He said the burns were only first degree and not too serious, except for the one that was more severe and would require a little more care.

The sea-sickness tablets seemed to do the most good; they relieved my headache somewhat.

Later Dr. Oatway left me in care of his colleague, Dr. B.C. Shaw. He also said that I should go to Medical Arts Centre in Winnipeg for blood tests. After Dr. Shaw had become acquainted with my case and after studying my burns, he gave me an anti-bacterial skin cleanser and an ointment.

Meanwhile the news of my encounter with the unknown object had spread throughout the city.

One of the people who took a special interest in the case was Barry Thompson of the APRO. After hearing my story he stated his belief that the craft was not an earthly creation. He persuaded me to take blood and radiation tests. I was grateful to Mr. Thompson because he was the first person who took my story seriously. He showed me that he knew quite a lot about such matters.

Other people I talked to were sceptical, but I don't blame them for I would have had doubts myself if someone else told me the same story.

Soon the telephone calls began. It seemed that everyone in Winnipeg wanted information about the UFO that I had seen. In my state of health I could not answer all the calls so my son Mark took up the task.

Many calls were from people who were sympathetic to my situation and I was grateful to them. I only regret that I could not remember all their names.

However, a number of names do linger in my memory. There was Mary Lou Armstrong of the University of Colorado, officials of the BBC and CBC, Prof. James McDonald of the University of Tucson, representatives of the *Winnipeg Free Press* and the *Winnipeg Tribune* and many others.

During this time my health made little progress. The most interesting thing was that I did not feel hungry. I had no desire to eat, and I continued to lose weight. I started making a chart and kept a record of the state of my health.

The news of what I had seen was spreading rapidly around the world. Articles appeared in newspapers and other publications. Some accounts gave validity to my story, others were quite sceptical.

I was afraid, I think, of ridicule more than anything else. Press investigations did not stop at my own home. Reporters went out to my friends and neighbours asking if they thought I was a stable person, whether I drank a lot, and whether I was the type who bragged and boasted a lot.

Then came the official investigations. The RCMP and the RCAF. Men whom I did not know and never expected to meet came to my door. They too had many questions to ask. What was my domestic life like? Why was I in the woods at the time? Somehow people seemed to have genuine interest in my experience, and I enjoyed talking to them.

I was amused by some people who came to quiz me. One could read their characters clearly just by the type of questions they asked. Some would say: "Why didn't you run?", or "Why didn't you enter the craft?", or "Weren't you afraid? I would have been!"

By evening following the incident, I was totally exhausted. I could talk to people no longer. I refused to answer the telephone. I tried to break off contact with the outside world.

This action only succeeded in creating discontent amongst the public. I began to be regarded as an ignorant anti-social creature. My detractors and critics could not know how I felt, could not appreciate what I was going through. They just couldn't know...

A soldier who has taken part in a battle, who has seen death and suffering can tell his story, and no matter how true it may be or how much emotion he may put into it, there will still be an element of disbelief in the listener. The masses cannot understand an individual. They listen, pass it on and forget it. This is how it was in my case. No one knew what I was going through.

During the next few days I saw Dr. Oatway and Dr. Shaw, radiologist Dr. T. D. Craddock, and a skin specialist, Dr. S. S. Berger.

On May 22 Mr. Thompson, in consultation with Dr. Craddock sent me to the national atomic research centre at Pinawa, Manitoba. I was examined for radiation. After the examination I was told that I was not suffering from radiation and was in no danger. Slowly my health improved.

THE SEARCH AND THE FIND

On June 4 Dr. Roy Craig of the University of Colorado and John Fried of *Life Magazine* called upon me. Together with Mr. Thompson, we went to Falcon Lake to try and find the site where the craft had landed.

Nature changes quickly at that time of the year and the forest was very much different now than it had been when I was there before. We searched and searched in vain.

I was sorry that our trip was unsuccessful, but there was nothing we could have done about it.

The same thing happened later when the members of the RCAF under Squadron Leader P. Bissky and the RCMP went with me to search for the spot.

We even used a helicopter, but it was no use. It seemed as if the place had disappeared from the face of the earth. The men who came with me were disenchanted. I made up my mind that sooner or later I'll find the spot and solve this mystery once and for all.

As my health improved, other reports of sightings turned up. A 13-year-old girl from Winnipeg, Darlene Bagley, reported seeing a similar thing. She made a sketch of it. Her sketch was not unlike the one I had made.

Then I heard about two boys seeing something near Falcon Lake about noon on May 20, the day of my experience with the object.

I found that within four weeks before and after my seeing the object there were at least 20 reported sightings in the area.

Slowly I tried to forget the events that had taken place. I returned to work and tried to get things back to normal.

Then on Sunday, June 10, three weeks after the day in Falcon Lake, I felt an itching in my chest. When I looked I noticed a number of blisters high up on my chest near the throat and a V-shaped rash that ran from the middle of my chest up to my ears.

I went to Dr. Shaw immediately. He examined me, took pictures and gave me some medication. It had no effect on the rash, and after a few days he sent me to Dr. Berger. I saw him for four weeks. During this time he gave me several treatments and the trouble disappeared.

On June 23 I contacted Mr. G.A. Hart, an electronic engineer in Winnipeg. He had offered me help earlier. I knew that he went to the Falcon Lake area quite frequently, so I asked him if I may accompany him some time and perhaps search for the landing site.

He not only took me there but helped me in the search. I looked throughout the woods checking rocks I had seen before, examining chips I had made in the stone and finally, after six hours, we came upon the spot.

Our greatest surprise was to see very plainly the outline of the ship on the ground where it had landed six weeks earlier.

We found the remains of my shirt at the scene along with the tape measure I lost that day. We placed the articles in plastic bags, gathered some samples of rock and earth from the area and took some pictures of the spot.

We also discovered that branches of trees in the area where the craft came down had withered away and died, while all around the trees were flourishing normally.

After looking around briefly, we returned to Falcon Lake, marking our way clearly so we could find the spot again.

Back in Winnipeg, I told Mr. Thompson and Sqd.-Ld.

Bissky that we had found the spot. On July 2 Corporal Davis and Constable J. Zacharias of the RCMP in Winnipeg came and took me to Falcon Lake. There we met Mr. Hunt, Mr. D. Thompson and Sqd.-Ld. Bissky. Together we went to the spot, took more pictures and samples and made more tests. They said there was some radiation but not enough to be dangerous.

Mr. Stewart Hunt of the National Department of Health and Welfare and Mr. D. Thompson of the provincial health department came to me later and with the members of the RCMP and the RCAF gave me a report on the samples.

Mr. Hunt told me the earth analysis showed radiation. He took Geiger counter readings in my house, but apart from the earth I had sent in, no further radiation was discovered. They promised to return for more tests.

Later in the week I went to see Dr. Berger because the rash had returned to my face. He again treated it.

At last the investigation was over. All there is to do is to wait for the final results, but I feel that they will never be made public.

Samples of earth and rock were also sent to Colorado University and to APRO. Accounts of the events mentioned appeared in magazines throughout the U.S. and Canada.

So far there is no official word. Perhaps our scientists are ashamed to admit that somewhere there is an intelligence and technology greater than ours.

As for the Government, it is possible that they are afraid that they will cause national panic if they reveal all they know, but it seems to me that they should say something definite.

The public had a right to know whether this thing came from our planet or from another world, whether it was friendly or harmful. People should be told what it was all about.

EPILOGUE OR INTERLUDE?

On September 21, just five months after my encounter with the craft at Falcon Lake, another strange thing happened.

I was on the roof of the Inland Cement Co., where I work. It started as a burning sensation around my neck and chest. At first it felt as a bee sting, but the pain was too intense and covered too great an area.

I went down to the first aid room to have the affliction examined. The pain grew worse and my throat began to feel like it was burning. My body began to swell. Tearing off my shirt, I noticed large red spots in the same place where the burns from the ship had been before.

The superintendent came in. After seeing what had happened he took me to a doctor immediately. In the next 15 minutes my body had turned violet. The swelling progressed so quickly that I could not take off my shirt again. My companion could not look at me, he kept turning away. My face must have looked horrible.

My hands looked as if they had been inflated with air – like a balloon, and I could feel my strength weakening. My vision was failing and I could make only dim outlines of things. The room was spinning around and I felt myself fading out into unconsciousness. I felt somebody lifting me onto a bed, but I was not aware of what was happening.

Later I was taken to Misericordia Hospital for observation. By nine p.m. that evening the symptoms began to disappear, my strength was returning and I began to feel better. I was released from the hospital at noon the following day, and all the swelling and marks had disappeared.

Doctors at the hospital said the swelling was the result of some allergy, but it seemed rather strange that the spots appeared in the same places where the UFO had left its marks.

33

On September 30 I returned to the place where the craft had landed – to see if there was any other changes. I could not believe what I saw.

The leaves in the area looked as if they had been sprayed with some killing chemical. All were withered and dead. No vegetation grew within a 50 feet radius of the landing site. The area where the craft had touched down was still visible.

I took more pictures, also a Geiger counter reading. It indicated a radiation count of 400 milliRoentgen.

I decided to return to the spot next May, one year after the sighting, to see if any changes have occurred and to see if the site is still discernable.

With regard to my health, I have been able to gather certain theories from various doctors and scientists as to the nature and source of the disturbances, their effects and any possible future results owing to the experience. One official said that my shirt and body was burned by ultrasonic waves, while another feels that it was a thermal reaction caused by a blast of hot air under pressure.

Radiologists have said that radiation found at the scene was a product of nuclear fission, like that emitted from an atomic reactor.

Another doctor said there were indications of the presence of the gamma rays which might have caused the burns and the immediate deterioration of food in my stomach which would have caused the awful stench I had experienced.

Yet another interesting observation showed that the amount of blood lymphocytes in the blood stream dropped from the normal 25 per cent to 16 per cent and finally returned to normal some four weeks after the sighting.

A federal report said that contact with the radiation may have caused or may yet cause blood cancer – leukemia.

Now that all seems to have ended as far as the events and after-effects are concerned, I would like to say that the burns and suffering I had endured were not caused by any aggressive moves of the craft of its occupants, as far as I can see.

The contact I had with the ship was of my own choosing and I was burned by the exhaust of the craft as it took off. Probably, if I stayed farther away from the craft I would not have been burned or suffered in any other way.

As a result, I offer this warning to all who may also encounter such a craft: keep away from it far enough to protect yourself and take all precautions against similar reactions.

THE END

PART 3

When They Appeared

By Stan Michalak

CHAPTER 1

The Basement

On May 20, 1967, the day it all started, I moved from my parents' bedroom into the basement. It was not emancipation. At the ripe age of nine, I hadn't given a change of scene much thought, and the basement was not finished, although we had talked about it since moving to Winnipeg just two years before. The transplant also took place very late in the evening on a Saturday and did not follow any particular plan, which was very unusual considering my mother always had a plan or, if not, she made it appear that every little thing we did received her full consideration. This time, she did not appear to be her usual assured self.

My father was sick. Or, at least, this is what I was told. Something had happened to him while he was away prospecting at Falcon Lake. The full extent of his injuries and the circumstances that brought him to this point were withheld from me for now. I figured that my parents' bedroom would become a sick room where Mom would nurse my Dad back to health and that there simply would be no room for me, though I feared that it wasn't just a matter of room – whatever illness my father had contracted had to be serious enough to warrant this sudden eviction. And it did not feel temporary.

My older brother Mark was to pick up my father at the bus station. Dad had called in the afternoon, and even as she bustled about the kitchen preparing dinner, my mother was visibly tense. Our meal, eaten hurriedly, was not accompanied by the usual banter, and we didn't linger like we always did over tea or coffee. When Mark left on his errand in our old '57 Ford Meteor, I wasn't told that there would be a stop at Misericordia Hospital's emergency room before he and Dad came home.

We moved to Winnipeg from Regina in the summer of 1965. Dad had found an excellent job at the Inland Cement Company as an industrial mechanic. In time, his employer would assist him in obtaining his millwright's ticket, which would open doors for him in the years to come and ensure that our little family never wanted for much. Despite the comfort of knowing that Dad had a good job, we weren't what anyone would call well off. I had a very sharp sense of that when I was enrolled in grade two at Queenston School. River Heights at that time was a neighbourhood of contrasts. As the son of a blue-collar worker, I fit into the bottom socio-economic half of the student population but somehow managed to rub elbows with a few kids who came from the wealthier side of the tracks. I suppose that we, being kids, tended not to notice these things, although I clearly remember playing with some of my classmates in their spacious Wellington Crescent homes and marvelling at their toy collections.

My brother Mark and sister Eva were students at the University of Manitoba – he in Engineering and she at the Faculty of Arts. Our family followed a certain pattern when it came to education: parochial elementary schools followed by private schools. For me, it was St. John Brebeuf for grades three to eight with high school at St. Paul's. That I would attend a Jesuit-run private boys' school was never in doubt. It was a paradigm established by my brother who graduated from Campion College in Regina, and, what was good enough for him...

How I spent those evening hours on that Saturday in May until Dad and Mark came home remains a blank. I hadn't been told of my new sleeping arrangements yet and knew only that Mark had gone to pick up our father. When they arrived, I was not there to greet them, and I have no recollection of Dad's condition at that moment nor did I appreciate the gravity of the situation. I do recall staying in our backyard after dark, long after my normal curfew, and coming into the house to discover that events had preceded me and that this day was going to change my family in a way I could not have imagined.

Mark had already begun moving my bed and my belongings into the basement when I came in. In between stepping into and out of the master bedroom while issuing instructions to Mark, my mother seemed to be directing traffic and tending to my Dad. This is how I learned of my change of scene: in snippets, hastily delivered by Mom while she instructed Mark, made tea and hustled into and out of the bedroom which, when I could catch a glimpse, was dimly lit. I was given the news in hushed tones that Dad was sick and was told to accompany Mark to the basement and set up my sleeping arrangements. It only took a few moments before I was in the basement with Mark deciding where the bed would go and how we would accommodate things like a dresser and lamp. At any other time, this would have been an interesting adventure for a nine-year old boy. It was way past my bedtime and it seemed to me that what was going on upstairs had granted me a sort of special dispensation. Yet, the tension in the house was so palpable that when Mark went up the stairs, all I was left with was fear.

For me, basements had always been scary. In Regina, we lived in a cavernous three-storey house with renters living in a full suite on the second floor and a tenant in an attic suite on the third. Our front entrance opened into a large hallway with a staircase to the right and a door leading to the basement under the stairs across from the main entry to our portion of the house – the main floor. In our part of the house, a cellar door off the kitchen gave us access to the basement – a back way down – reached by a set of stairs that were so steep, they forced one to practically climb them like a ladder. I took a nose-dive down those stairs more than a few times as a toddler, each time giving myself one injury or another. When I wasn't tumbling down the back stairs, the basement was where I could interact with our tenants who came down to do their laundry. It was also where my brother had his bedroom. I had visions of one day having this same kind of retreat – a "boy cave" where I could play with my friends and do things outside of my mother's supervision. But when the lights were off and there were no friendly faces, the basement was a spooky home for the kind of scary monsters that live in a child's imagination. As fate would have it, our new home in Winnipeg also came with a basement.

As I sat on my transplanted bed in the dim glow of a single lamp on a makeshift night table, I couldn't help but feel that while I was expected to be a strong and responsible nine-year old while the rest of my family dealt with something truly disturbing that I didn't understand, I wasn't up to the task. When Mom finally came to tuck me in, she offered comforting words but gave me no further clues about what was happening. It took a long time for me to even consider falling asleep although it had to be well past midnight.

The glow from the main floor lit the stairway. Like so many other tiny post-war bungalows in this neighbourhood, the stairs to the basement began in the hallway between the front entrance hall and the kitchen. To reach the basement, you stepped down four stairs to the side door landing, turned right and continued down eight more stairs that took a further right turn at the bottom.

I crept out of bed and, guided by the light spilling down from the hall, made my way to the stairs and climbed them silently to the landing, where I discovered that the hallway acted like a sound tunnel, bringing all conversation in the house right to this point. And despite trying to keep their discussion at a low volume, what Mom was saying to my brother and sister in the dining room was clear as a bell. If I sat still, I had a front-row seat on that landing, and I could scamper back down the stairs quietly if I heard anyone coming.

As I sat there on the stairs in my pyjamas, my fear of basements disappeared that night. In its place, a seed of profound bewilderment was planted which grew each time I eavesdropped on conversations from my covert listening post.

Mom's voice from the dining room carried with it the sounds of concern but also resignation, as if she had come to terms with what was happening. It was the voice she used when she had no explanation for something and that our only course was to accept whatever transpired because "that's how it is." As far as my brother and sister were concerned, this was not an opening for a discussion, merely a statement of affairs as Mom saw it.

Being afraid of basements was nothing compared with what was to come.

CHAPTER 2

My Injured Father

When I awoke that Sunday morning, the noises and smells from the kitchen suggested Mom was making breakfast. She had tried to give Dad some eggs and dry toast, but he couldn't keep them down. On my visit to the bathroom, I noticed the door to the bedroom was closed but, while brushing my teeth, I heard the door open and close and caught a few of the words that passed between Mom and Dad. There was something about pain medication, reference to a glass of tea, words about washing or bathing, and then my name was mentioned. At this, I froze, anxious to hear what was being said but only hearing hushed murmurs. When the door opened and closed again, I ventured out of the bathroom.

Breakfast was going to be a favourite of mine – loosely scrambled eggs with bits of ham and chopped green onion. Mark and Eva had already eaten and were going about their own affairs. As I ate at the dining room table, Mom came in and sat down with a glass of tea in her hand and explained that Dad was very sick, that he had an accident while in the bush at Falcon Lake, that he had been burned, that he had visited the hospital yesterday evening, and that he just needed some rest. I was told that I could see him later in the day if Dad was up to it and if the pills he was taking didn't make him too drowsy. While I had questions, it was obvious from her manner that this was all the explanation I was going to get for now, and it would have to be enough.

If the eggs had any flavour in them at all, I couldn't remember. I finished in silence while Mom went about cleaning up after breakfast. I tried to recall what I had overheard the night before but nothing made any sense to me.

When he came to Canada in 1949, Dad worked on a farm in southern Saskatchewan and grew to love the Canadian wilderness. His native Poland, ravaged by war and then in the hands of the Soviet regime, was once a place where he enjoyed roaming the fields and forests. When war broke out and the Polish military was defeated, Dad was forced to abandon his regular army career and join the ranks of the partisans. The next eight years were endless danger and misery. It was a chapter of his life that could fill an entire book. After coming to the new world, he renounced the native land for which he had once fought, adopted the Canadian way of life and began his lifelong love of nature and the outdoors. And there was so much of it here.

His work on a farm near Lafleche was part of the Canadian government's sponsorship program in which he had enrolled on entering the country. He was a farm hand, living with a French-Canadian family on the prairie, putting in long hours with the crops and livestock and spending his free time in the woods and meadows of southern Saskatchewan. In time, he began taking courses in mechanics so that he could repair farm machinery when it was required. He also took an interest in the country's hidden resources after he was told the hills and streams of this country were brimming with precious metals and gems. The interest led to a series of courses on geology, a subject that quickly became a passion. I recall countless times when he would stoop down, pick up what I considered to be an ordinary rock, and tell me the secrets that it held.

From last night's overheard conversation in the dining

room and from what I already knew, I confirmed that Dad had decided to spend most of the Victoria Day long weekend in Falcon Lake – a lake resort community about 90 minutes east of Winnipeg on the fringes of the Canadian Shield. He had started this annual trek last year after we had visited that part of Manitoba on a few car trips to Falcon Lake and further east to Kenora. To my Dad, the Canadian Shield represented a geological paradise. This was a land of granite and quartz and, he hoped, nickel and gold. It was so different from the flatlands of south Saskatchewan that it drew him like a moth to a flame. After many visits, a collection of rocks began to grow in our basement, filling several wooden crates, each sample clearly labelled and all cross-referenced to a map of the area. While I didn't realize it at the time, he had even staked several claims in the woods just north of the Trans-Canada Highway at Falcon Lake. If there was any precious metal in that part of the province, Dad was determined to find it.

I remember holding large chunks of quartz, some of them incredibly beautiful, while Dad described the formation of crystals, the geological forces at work and the by-products of that creation. In tiny fissures, here and there, I could sometimes glimpse a yellow streak of gold. Even when gold was not present, Dad would proudly draw out another sample and show it to me like it was a precious gem. And many were – at least to me. A piece of beautiful rose quartz that had been chipped away from its mother-rock by my father after he had hiked for many hours to find it had to be precious. I found it compelling that Dad had gone to all this trouble to harvest this tiny piece of the Canadian Shield. It wasn't until much later in my life I realized that my passion for so many things I eventually pursued was born while sitting at my Dad's knee looking at rocks and calculating how much effort had been required to produce this collection.

I never got the impression that his love of geology was

an obsession despite the passion he showed for it. He went to work each day and spent time with his family. He was also an oil painter – something he had started in Poland and now pursued with renewed ambition. Canvasses bloomed on our walls, both in our first home in Regina and now in Winnipeg.

We spent a good deal of time in the outdoors as a family picnicking, hiking and enjoying nature. I knew he spent time with his "rocks" (a term coined by my mother), but it never struck me that this was time wasted, nor did it appear to be taking time away from anything else.

His green haversack was always packed and ready. I know because I snooped on more than one occasion. In it, he kept his rock hammer, goggles to shield his eyes from chips, a pair of stout rubber gauntlets, a compass, several heavy canvas sacks to bring back samples, a notebook, tape measure, and a few clothing items. When he planned an excursion, he would add food, water, a thermos of coffee, and he was off.

Now, this seemingly benign hobby had hurt him. Of all the pursuits in his life and all the dangers he had faced during the war, he was injured by a hobby. And, not just a minor injury, something that had sent him to the emergency room, banished me to the basement, and something that had my mother concerned.

In addition to being scared, I was now confused.

Later that day, I heard Mom and Dad talking and I realized the bedroom door was open. When she emerged, my mother told me that I could see him but only briefly as he was still drowsy, weak and not eating solid food.

The curtain was drawn back to let in some daylight and the room was brighter than it had been yesterday. Dad was propped up on some pillows with a glass of tea in his hand. On the nightstand, a jar of cream, a bottle of pills, a box of tissues and a plate with some cold rye toast competed for space. He was wearing striped blue pyjamas and his face was drawn and pale.

When I walked in to the bedroom, a wall of odour struck me so hard I stopped in my tracks. It was the stink of sulphur overlaid with ozone – the smell that comes out of a burning electric motor that has overheated. Together they formed a miasma of sickness, of wrongness – so much so that I froze in place. Dad opened his eyes, noticed me and gestured that I should come closer. He patted the bed – an invitation for me to sit. His voice was hoarse and I spotted bandages on his upper chest. The smell seemed to be coming from him – from the very pores of his skin.

He told me not to worry, assured me that he would be fine and reminded me to listen to my mother and do what she said. He mentioned nothing about the smell, or the pain, or the burns, or the cause... nothing at all.

It wasn't enough. Not nearly enough. While all the questions I had began to jostle in line eager to spill out, I stayed mute. He patted my hand, a gesture that this audience had come to an end, and I left the room in silence. Rather than offering a comforting hug (which I desperately needed), Mom told me to go downstairs and help my brother who was improving my new bedroom and dividing the space in the basement to accommodate his study area.

To fit our family into this tiny home, Mark slept on a hide-a-bed in the living room which became the sofa during the day. His clothes occupied an armoire in the basement, and a desk and shelves had been set up there so that he could study. Eva had been given the main-floor bedroom at the back of the house – an addition built by the previous owner that pushed the square footage of our little house from 700 to just over 800 square feet. Out of necessity, Mark hung a set of blankets to partition the basement and give us privacy – for him, study space, and for me, a bedroom of sorts. Dad had made a little progress on the basement, putting up shelves and building DIY closets to store things. But it was, for the most part, an unfinished basement with a concrete floor. Mark even installed a homemade blackboard on the wall above his desk so that he could work on the advanced math that was part of his engineering courses. I often fell asleep to the click-clack sounds the chalk made on the board as Mark solved equations late into the night.

In the days to come, Mark would not only prepare for and pass his exams, he would also become our family's Horatio, the point man, the filter, the security guard, our spokesman and, at times, a much bigger big brother. At least, that's how he appeared to me then and for many years after.

For now, normalcy was being restored, but it was not going to last past that night.

My brother Mark, in his air cadet uniform, and my father, discuss the finer points of a scale model he has built in a photo from Regina dated 1963.

CHAPTER 3

The Story Hits the Paper

Later on Sunday, I was surprised to hear raised voices coming from my parents' bedroom. It was quite a contrast to the dim and quiet I had experienced earlier and Dad's voice sounded more robust, almost like his normal self. Mom and Dad were having a heated discussion – not exactly an argument, but it sounded serious enough for me to slink up the basement stairs to my listening post. At full speed, Polish, like so many European languages, takes on a heightened intensity and volume. My mother was clearly not willing to budge on her belief that what my father was proposing was not in anyone's best interests. For his part, Dad was arguing a moral position, stating that it was a duty and obligation to report what he had seen and the events that followed. What had he seen? And, why would he argue that he was obliged to report it... and to whom?

The discussion ended as so many did in our house: in mutual silence. Her heavy footsteps coming my way made me slip down the stairs before I could get caught. I heard her rummaging for the phone book in the entrance hall, then return to the bedroom with the phone, dragging the phone's extension cord along the hardwood floors.

Who they called and why was a mystery. From the basement I could hear voices but no conversation. I just knew that

Dad was on the phone for a very long time.

Later that evening the doorbell rang. My mother answered and there was some brief small talk at the door – a woman's voice. Then another voice joined in – a man's. Together they trooped down the hall and into my parents' bedroom. When Mom came downstairs to get me ready for bed, I knew that I would not be eavesdropping with her on guard; it felt as though she was keeping me away from the people in her bedroom. I didn't ask; she didn't tell. I fell asleep hearing the murmur of voices from upstairs.

Holiday Monday dawned for me as it did for every school-age kid – happy to not be going to school and ready for whatever would come. When I checked in with Dad, I found him to be as weak as before but with a slightly brighter disposition. He was still having trouble with solid food, so Mom had him drinking chicken broth from a mug. It was something, but I didn't think a man like my Dad would be able to carry on for long without eating. The room still had a peculiar odour – remnants of what I had smelled yesterday, but Mom attempted to clear the air by opening the bedroom window and letting in the spring breeze. As for last night's visitors, neither spoke a word about who they were or what was discussed.

Mom came and went, checking on Dad's progress with the broth and reminding him of when he was to take his next pill. I didn't know what they were, but the pills seemed to make him drowsy. The label on the bottle announced that they were from the Misericordia Hospital, so I assumed he had got them on Saturday evening. After a brief discussion about Dad seeing our family doctor, my mother hustled me out of the bedroom to give Dad a chance to rest.

As usual, Mark was enlisted to chauffeur Dad to our family doctor's office. On their return, the pills Dad had received from the Misericordia were discarded from the nightstand and my mother replaced them with two new bottles, both with the name of Dr. Oatway, our family doctor.

In later years, Mom kept a detailed journal of her own health and every single interaction with the medical community. Each medication she had been prescribed and every procedure or test was duly noted in a diary in great detail. While a lot of it was annotated in Polish, the diary became an incredible guide for medical staff each time she had to go to the hospital. In some cases, I'm willing to bet the notes were lifesavers.

My father, my brother Mark and sister Eva with me in the middle on the lawn in front of our Winnipeg house in the summer of 1967.

It's difficult to remember exactly when she began this habit, but I believe it was prompted by Dad's case. After settling Dad in bed, she started a chart of his medications, noted his weight and began to describe his daily intake of food and fluids, how many times and how much he urinated, and whether or not he was able to produce a stool. I marvelled at her attention to detail and, weeks later, I noted the chart covered several hand-written pages. She was then, and continued to be until his death in 1999, a very efficient nurse.

Nine-year olds don't read newspapers – at least, none of the nine-year olds I knew. And I was certainly no different. Up to that point, the newspaper was for adults and I got the news that they deemed a nine-year old should know. We had a black and white TV with rabbit ears on a rolling cart so that we could set it up in almost any room. Occasionally, especially Sunday evening, we watched TV together as a family. As for the news, that was not interesting to me.

Imagine my surprise when the afternoon edition of the *Winnipeg Tribune* arrived with the story "I Was Burned by UFO" across the top of the paper with a photo of my father holding his pyjama top open to reveal a pattern of dark dots across his upper chest. The reporter was Heather Chisvin, and I gathered that it was her voice I had heard last night in the front hall. Mom tried to keep the paper from me, but it was being passed back and forth among her, my brother and sister. When I could bear it no longer, all of my questions came pouring out. In the style I would recognize for years to come, Mom merely nodded towards the bedroom and told me to ask my father to explain.

He told me the story, and I'm sure he left out many pertinent details, but he covered enough ground that I formed a picture in my head of what he was telling me. My nine-year old imagination saw this UFO as a spaceship, piloted by aliens that had landed in the woods, burned my father, and disappeared. A spaceship! As the acronym explained, it was an

Unidentified Flying Object. But it just had to be a flying saucer, didn't it? What else looked like that? What else looked like the pictures I saw in those newspapers by the checkouts at the local Safeway store? What else could it be but the subject of so many science fiction comics and books and movies and TV shows?

I peppered my father with questions about size, shape, sound – anything that would make the story more real to me. At no time did I doubt his tale. He was my father after all, and I had never been given any opportunity to doubt that this man, who was a war hero to me, would be anything but forthright. He showed me the burns on his chest – an angry, red patch of blisters with scorched hair and a pattern of dark red dots as large as coins marching across his abdomen. He showed me the sketch he had made with all of his notes. Oh, yes! I could practically see the visitors stepping out and asking Dad to take them to his leader. He answered all of my questions and I would have asked more had Mom not come in and pointed out that he was growing weaker by the moment and that his hoarse voice should be a clue that he had said enough for one day. As I was shooed out the door, I was struck by one very odd exemption from the conversation. At no point in our chat did he say that he believed the craft to be from another world even though my boyish imagination had already come to that conclusion. When I pushed him to declare what he thought he saw, he would only say, "You tell me."

My brother Mark had been in the air cadets in Regina. Being ten years younger, I got to imagine myself in his shoes when I grew up. Naturally, his love of aviation became mine, something I carry to this very day. We both marvelled at the world of aero science and technology. He made scale models and put on his air cadet uniform once a week while I mimicked his paramilitary bearing. He often shared the latest aviation news with me, showing me photos of the newest jet aircraft. I remember going with Mark to the corner store in Regina to buy Creamsicles because inside every Creamsicle wrapper was an aviation collector card. I ate a lot of Creamsicles and collected a lot of cards. I still love the taste.

In all that enthusiasm about aviation, not once did I hear any discussion about the possibility of UFOs, nor did the family follow with any interest the stories that had started to appear regularly in newspapers and magazines probably as far back in time as the Roswell incident of 1947. The very thought of UFOs belonged in the realm of science fiction. It was the stuff of *Flash Gordon, War of the Worlds* and pulp novels. Nobody in our family gave it a second thought.

Now, science fiction had arrived at our very doorstep. It was convalescing in my parent's bedroom. It had left a mark on my father and, as these things go, it would mark our family for decades. Pandora's box had been opened because my father believed in a gesture of civic responsibility. It was something he and my mother would regret in years to come. We were naïve to think that a simple newspaper article would be the end of it. And, as it turned out, my father's trusting nature was his undoing. It would lead to years of frustration and forever change his character. And, it would test the rest of us like nothing else we had ever or would ever encounter. In a way, that UFO burned us all.

CHAPTER 4

The Bullying Begins

Having to go to school, I missed a lot of activity at the house over the next few weeks until summer break. I never guessed that a simple newspaper article would start such a storm, but I caught the first sprinkle of the showers to come almost as soon as I had returned to class. I had changed schools and was now in grade three at St. John Brebeuf school where I would remain until grade eight. The tough guys of the third grade singled me out during the very first recess of the day. They taunted me with questions to confirm that I was, indeed, the son of the UFO guy, then they carried on to bring any number of details into the rant including that I was a Polack and that my immigrant father was the janitor at a cement factory. They held me down and tried to pull up my jacket to see if I had green alien skin and, despite my struggles, I couldn't protect myself. My saviour on this day was my third-grade teacher, Marjorie Smith, who was out on recess duty, patrolling the schoolyard with an ever-present gaggle of girls surrounding her.

Some teachers stand out. I had a few at this elementary school whom I remembered with considerable fondness decades later. One of them was Marjorie Smith. Scattering the bullies before her like St. Patrick and the snakes, Mrs. Smith collected me, shooed away her gaggle and took me inside to an empty classroom where we sat and chatted while I cried – not from pain but from embarrassment. Not only had I gone from acceptable to a pariah in one day, I had been unable to stand up for myself and, to top all horrors, the girl I liked was in Mrs. Smith's orbit and witnessed my shame when the group came by. Mrs. Smith was familiar with the story in the paper and promised to be there for me whenever I needed her at the school. As it turned out, she not only watched over me, she became a good friend to my mother and remained so for many years, long after I had left to go on to high school. In many ways, she was responsible for allowing me to keep a measure of dignity that gave me the incentive to continue in that school. I needed that, because I would continue to be bullied on my way to and from school where even the long arms of Mrs. Smith couldn't reach.

I returned home in the afternoon, keeping a wary eye on any ambushes along the way, to find two strange men at the door. They were talking with Mark, who obviously was not letting them in. I quickly passed by, through the gate and inside the side door to hear the end of the conversation. The men were from the newspaper, although I don't recall which one. Mark had politely but firmly denied them a chance to talk with Dad. It was not the first visit from reporters that he deflected.

I learned that it had been a busy day at the house. A man identifying himself as a representative of the Aerial Phenomena Research Organization (APRO) in the United States had called ahead and spent the morning with Dad discussing the events of May 20. His name was Barry Thompson, and his card indicated he was with CAPRO (the Canadian wing of APRO). Nobody we knew had ever heard of such an organization, but it appeared that this group had long been following the various sightings and reports of UFO activity, not only in America but also around the world. Thompson would become a regular visitor, and he inserted himself whenever possible into the investigative events to come. We could not know at the time, but the legacy of Barry Thompson would do more harm than good.

Later that morning, the RCMP showed up. Mark ushered in two men: Corporal Davis and a Constable Zacharias. I missed the chance to hear what was said, although my eaves-

My mother and I dressed to go out in the summer of 1967.

dropping that evening produced some solid results as Mom and Dad compared notes about the events of the day. According to Mom, the officers seemed polite and basically wanted to check on the report that had been filed by Constable Solotki, an RCMP officer from the Falcon Beach detachment who had met Dad on the highway immediately following the incident. Their presence in our house had been sparked by Solotki's report, and the fact that it only took a day or two meant the RCMP were giving this more than just a passing glance.

From Mom's point of view, it was clear that Dad's conduct on the highway that day and Solotki's report painted a very negative picture. She was clearly dressing down Dad for making some bad choices while he reminded her that he had been injured and only thinking about what had happened to him and how it might affect others. He also mentioned Thompson, and pointed out that of all the people he had interacted with, including the RCMP, Thompson proved to be the most supportive. After all, Dad said, Thompson belonged to an organization that actually investigated and reported such events, so he had to have certain *bona fides*. And, he sounded happy to have chatted with Thompson before the RCMP interview. Mom was unconvinced, and pointed out that she did not trust Thompson… "There was just something about him…"

They had a brief exchange about Dad's prospecting and the nickel claims he had filed. This really brought up the heat of the discussion. Dad was adamant that all his hard work would not be in vain and that he would continue pursuing his hobby now that it appeared there may be some success. Mom would hear nothing of it. Dad's hobby would end there and then, and that was that. Their conversation ended when she correctly pointed out that Dad's fears about radiation poisoning and its effects on people near him might be unfounded anyway. I found out from Mark later that the day had not ended with the interview.

Mark had taken Mom and Dad to see another doctor that day, though I discovered that this was no ordinary physician but a radiologist who confirmed that Dad had not been injured by radioactivity. They took his hat and shirt for analysis and they, too, were found to be uncontaminated. My theory that aliens had fired some kind of laser death ray at him went out the window. Based on what my father had described, the burns were caused by a jet of gases that were hot enough to set his shirt and undershirt on fire. The whole radiation scare turned out to be a big red herring in the end.

Despite the clean bill of health, radiation would still rear its ugly head later on. When Dad was finally able to find the site, he brought back everything he had left there on May 20 in one bag along with a sample of the soil which did, indeed, show elevated radiation levels. So, naturally, everything in the bag got contaminated as well. He may have been an industrial mechanic, but he was no scientist. It was not the first time he would make a mistake that hung a cloud over his story. But, he wasn't the only one who made assumptions that muddied the tale. When traces of radiation were discovered at the site by "experts" who were sent there with Geiger counters, there was a flurry of activity that would later prove to be unnecessary.

According to everyone who actually examined him in a medical setting and at test facilities where actual scientists worked, radiation did not harm him, make him sick or infect him in a way that would haunt him later. Sure, there were issues with his white cell count and other factors in his blood, but the comment from one researcher that Dad had been exposed to gamma rays was not only laughable, it was absurd.

So, no alien death rays; good news for a nine-year old.

However, there was still a matter of the after-effects of the incident and the fact that Dad was weak, nauseated, couldn't hold down solid food, experienced headaches and fainting spells, and was losing weight. Mom figured it was about four, maybe five pounds a day at this rate, and implored him to try harder while she found something that would stay down. And there was the matter of the RCMP and how they would pursue this investigation.

Late into the evening, the phone rang incessantly. Mark was there for every call, fielding simple questions but basically blowing off reporters who were intent on getting direct quotes from the victim himself or, at the very least, his wife. Mom, of course, would have absolutely no part of it. Barry Thompson had offered to become the family's spokesperson, but since he could not be there 24 hours a day, the task remained in Mark's hands.

My sister, Eva, was the only one in our family who seemed to stay clear of the controversy and reporters. She had always been musically gifted and had a lovely voice. She was busy singing professionally at the CBC in the evenings and pursuing her Arts degree during the day at the University of Manitoba. When asked if she knew this man who saw the UFO, she said she didn't know anything about UFOs, only that her father was very ill as a result of this incident. She certainly cared about what had happened to Dad and the fallout it had generated, but she focused her attention on the family and her studies and gave little time to the outsiders who seemed bent on annoying us.

For my part, I continued to explore cunning new ways to avoid being harassed on my way to and from school. One day, my clever plans failed and I was accosted by several kids, most of them my age; a few boys were a little older.

Enter my second saviour.

When my mother came to Canada with Mark and Eva in 1957, she was immediately thrust into the lives of the French-Canadian farm families with whom my Dad had found a home, employment and friendship. That they greeted her warmly was of little consequence. She was new to this world, had no English, no real housekeeping skills, and two pre-teen children. In a short time, she was also pregnant with me. It was clear that life in a remote prairie village would not do, and my father wisely moved his little family to Regina.

Gradually, the life of a "big" city agreed with her and Mom began to bloom. In a fairly short time, with the example of my Dad's renouncement of his homeland, she came to recognize that assimilation in this country meant cutting ties with Poland, other than correspondence with her family. So we rarely, if ever, spent any time searching out the Polish immigrant community. Mark fit in very quickly, my sister took longer to adapt, and I, the first-born Canadian in the family, slipped into the life quite naturally.

In Winnipeg, Dad met Henryk Lorenc, a fellow Pole who worked at the cement plant and who would later become quite an icon in the city's Polish-Canadian community. Henryk's family would all contribute to the celebration of their Polish roots: he eventually co-founded *Folklorama*, Winnipeg's premier cultural festival. For now, we were happy to have met another Polish-speaking family and spent some wonderful times with this couple and their kids who were about the same ages as my brother and sister.

As for me, I was happy then to be un-Polish, adopting a more Canadian persona. When the language of the house was Polish, I understood, but answered in English. It was a tug-of-war that would continue until I discovered late in life that I truly missed celebrating that heritage.

Which brings us back to my second saviour.

On the day I was cornered, I had no chance. We were far enough away from school, and I had made the fatal mistake of choosing a wide route home that took me close to the open field and railroad tracks that still run through the neighbourhood. When confronted by several boys, I thought my goose was truly cooked. Suddenly, from nowhere, a boy several years older than any of us barged into the crowd and started swinging. Within minutes, there were kids running in all directions while this older boy took great delight in giving them a good pounding and calling out a string of obscenities in heavily accented English. His name was Jurek Bobkowski. He was a fellow Pole. Yes, when it mattered and my skin was on the line, I was as Polish as all get out.

Jurek lived on my street but much further south, almost at the end of the street, in a tiny house with his parents and little sister Diana. He was eleven or twelve – practically a teenager – and had a rough edge to him. He was a student at my school and his English was good, but there was an accent that I found very interesting. We started using Polish between us as our own personal communication code so that others at school would not know what we were about. And, as part of our ruse, he maintained a cool detachment from me at school unless I raised the alarm.

He saved me that day and on other days, and not only would he continue to be there for me in the months ahead, his family and mine became good friends. Even after they moved to British Columbia many years later and I lost contact with the family, his mother Halina stayed in touch with my mother right up until Mom died in 2015. She was a tried and true friend and, for a while, Jurek was mine.

It was a comfort to know that bullying might not be as big a problem as I had experienced, but the harassment never really stopped until the publicity died down years later and we resumed a fairly normal life. In time, I learned from my Dad how to take care of myself in a tight spot. Mrs. Smith faded into the background and Jurek went on to high school and another province, but I will always be grateful that two saviours showed up so soon to give me a leg up on the fallout that was affecting our family.

CHAPTER 5

The Relentless Media

Whenever I mention the "day they appeared," I'm asked to what am I referring. Is it the UFOs I'm talking about? Most certainly not. It is the endless stream of reporters, well-wishers, flim-flam artists, odd folks, interested parties, government agency representatives, the authorities, investigators of all types and just simple nutcases who washed up on our doorstep like a never-ending tsunami. On the flip side, we made some long-lasting friendships with people who were aware of the notoriety my father had attracted but chose to be supportive and enjoy the company of our family regardless of how they may have felt about what Dad had endured or what was at the source of it.

One such couple was Marty and June McGregor. Jurek's father, a local architect, introduced them to my family. Marty and his wife enlarged our family's social circle in a very meaningful way: they were not of Polish descent – far from it. Marty, a professional engineer, was very interested in Dad's story and chose to take a pragmatic approach. Rather than blindly believe the encounter had been extraterrestrial, he was interested in the physical aspects of it and the effect it had on Dad and my family. In the months and years to come, Marty and June became good friends, and Marty was often the voice of reason and caution when events tumbled along at a rate my father was not prepared to handle.

Reporters continued to dog our steps. The steps of our house were littered with spent flash bulbs that Mark collected and threw in the trash. I was followed to school one day by a man who was very insistent that I speak to him about Dad, as if what I had to say on the matter was remotely newsworthy. It was only when I crossed into the schoolyard that he wisely chose to back off.

It is important to remember the era in which this case occurred. There were no home computers, no digital cameras, and no portable recording devices. Newspaper reporters came armed with pads and pencils, usually with photographers in tow who were determined to get a shot of Dad or anyone else who poked their head out our front door or pulled aside the living room curtains. As for TV news, the equipment required to do an on-site interview filled a small van. It was rare to have a TV crew show up unannounced; they quickly discovered that the amount of work required to set up a location shoot only to get nothing from it wasn't worth the effort. We had such an invasion, but only once. I remember watching Mark one evening as he gathered to-go coffee cups, cigarette butts and other litter from our front lawn after an all-day vigil by one of our local TV stations.

At first, Dad was willing to cooperate and tell his story. As I sat in my stairwell, I heard debates between my parents about which TV station was worthy or which reporter deserved to get an audience. Our relationship with the *Winnipeg Tribune* had surpassed Heather Chisvin and now included Peter Warren, a man who would one day become a well-known if not well-loved radio talk show host. Trading on the relationship already established by the fact that the *Tribune* had carried the initial story, Warren convinced Dad that a one-on-one interview was the best thing to take the story to the next level; Warren wanted more on the man at the centre of this storm.

Within days of the first story, Warren had Dad meet him at the St. Regis Hotel where he had booked a private room. It was anonymous, neutral ground, and the two were sequestered for some time. I recall seeing how incredibly tired Dad was when the taxi brought him home. The follow-up stories that appeared were, in my family's estimation, fairly well balanced, although, like with anything the media did at the time, there were many gaps in the information about what kind of person my father was, and the quotes Warren chose were tailored to fit the narrative. Warren became a staunch defender of Dad's story largely based on that one-day interview. It seems the things they talked about that did not make the final cut were significant enough for Warren to form a strong opinion. Years later, Warren would go on record to say that he believed the man he had interviewed – not necessarily that the incident had involved extraterrestrial visitors, but that Dad was telling the truth that the events happened as he described them. It's a pity the articles didn't fully explore that part of their conversation.

Mark's vigilance went beyond day-to-day visitations. In those first few weeks, other news agencies began to hover. We were pestered by phone calls at all hours. First, it was the local news: papers, radio and TV. Then the story was being picked up nationally, then internationally. The big three American networks all chimed in: NBC, CBS and ABC. One night, the phone rang, and Mark answered the way all people do when they get calls at 3:00 a.m. – by asking if the caller knew what time it was. It was the BBC. Our little story had made it overseas.

Naturally, all this media attention reached the desks of non-news agencies. As a kid, I couldn't fathom the effects of a story of these proportions and the number or variety of people who would be reading it. It did not take very long for the authorities to step in.

CHAPTER 6

RCMP Officers Visit Often

While I was in school on Wednesday, the RCMP came back to our house. In an interview that lasted the afternoon, Corporal Davis calmly and methodically walked Dad through all of the events of the Victoria Day long weekend while a tape recorder ran. I remember seeing Davis for the first time that day when I came home from school. I caught only a brief portion of their conversation after the formal part of the interview had ended and, from my spot on the landing, I realized I had missed a good deal. It was frustrating that I had to go to school while all the really interesting things happened outside my watch.

I liked Davis from the moment I was briefly introduced. He was tall and good looking (my mother commented more than once that he was a handsome man – a sentiment that went over the head of a simple nine-year old). I did note that he was what I considered the epitome of a Mountie: ramrod straight, slim and with a soft-spoken voice that came out in measured phrases. He seemed kind and considerate and was very gracious with Mom who served him coffee and dainties while he interviewed Dad. In the weeks to come, I looked forward to seeing him and always asked whether he would be joining the groups of people who gathered at our house on the seemingly endless expeditions to Falcon Lake.

67

What I could not know then was that the RCMP already had a growing file on my father. It had started the day of the incident when Dad approached the RCMP on the highway near Falcon Lake. Constable Solotki of the Falcon Beach detachment had already filed an incident report and, after the story made the paper, it was probably hustled up the administrative chain to the D Division Headquarters of the RCMP in Winnipeg which sent Davis and Zacharias for a follow-up interview on Tuesday and prompted this re-visit today.

The initial report by Solotki did not become available to us until years later. Based on their discussions yesterday and today, it seemed that Davis was intent on clarifying the conclusions Solotki had reached in his initial report: that Dad may have been drunk, that there was too much information being withheld, that there was, perhaps, more to this than met the eye.

When I finally did read the report many years later, it was clear that Solotki had very little regard for this strange man who had flagged him down on the highway. The subsequent RCMP reports were much more thorough and balanced and, even though they correctly pointed out the mistakes Dad made throughout the investigation, there was really nothing in them to disprove the events of that day in May.

That the RCMP appeared serious about the case and was willing to put in the time was obvious by the number of visits officers made to the house. We saw a lot of Davis and Zacharias over the weeks to come. They were back on Thursday and anxious for Dad to take them to Falcon Lake and revisit the site. My clandestine listening had confirmed that Mom was adamant that Dad cooperate as fully as possible, though she repeated her concern that he was in no shape to go gallivanting off into the bush on any kind of trek with anyone. It was a position confirmed by Dr. Oatway who told the RCMP that my father was not well enough yet to accompany them to Falcon Lake. For his part, Dad was willing to assist; something in his character demanded that he respect the authority of our federal police force. But Barry Thompson cautioned him about doing so in the face of being charged by police. Thompson had somehow convinced Dad that he needed an advocate, someone who could shield him from any attempts by any authority to disprove his claims or, worse, to find him liable for mischief, and that he, Thompson, was the man for the job.

My evening listening sessions revealed to me that a problem was developing. Dad firmly defended what Thompson was proposing, claiming that this man had his best interests at heart. My mother was not so sure. And, in the months ahead, it became increasingly more difficult to determine which one of the dozens of people involved could be trusted, believed or relied on and, in the end, she stated categorically that the well being of the family came first. Her argument clearly touched a nerve.

When war broke out in Poland in 1939, Dad was serving with the intelligence section of the military police. His beat took him to the eastern reaches of the country along the Polish-Ukrainian border where he was responsible for uncovering covert activities by elements of pro-Soviet fifth columnists who had been smuggling arms and generally becoming a nuisance to good order and discipline. He came from a police and military family. His father was chief of police in the small town in which he was born.

When hostilities opened with Nazi Germany, the military was assailed from both sides: the German juggernaut in the west and the growing menace of Communist Russia from the east. Once the regular Polish army had been defeated, serving members went underground and started factions of partisans to fight the Nazi occupiers. It would have been a very simple prospect except that there were two wings of partisans operating in occupied Poland: the Home Army, loyal to the

My mother and father's wedding portrait in Poland following World War II.

Polish government-in-exile and composed of ex-army members, and; the People's Army – Communist supporters who were armed and organized by Soviet Russia. Dad's loyalty was tested throughout the war but he never wavered, even when it was discovered that his father had been one of tens of thousands of Poles who had been arrested by the Soviets and who perished, either in the labour camps of Siberia or in mass executions in the east of Poland.

Dad believed in loyalty and honour. When the allies defeated Nazi Germany in 1945, and my father was released after a year and a half in the Gross-Rosen concentration camp, he remained an active operative for the exiled Polish government, this time targeting the Soviets who had invaded from the east and "liberated" Poland. The country was now a Soviet state, the government-in-exile declared irrelevant, and any member of the Home Army who was not prepared to toe the party line was considered an outlaw and hunted down. In this post-war mess, Dad began to question his blind loyalty to a country that had given up everything for which he stood.

His one escape from the political pressures of the time was his marriage to my mother, who survived 14 months in the Ravensbruck concentration camp. They had met through her father, a man Dad had been instrumental in saving from the Nazi death squads. They married in 1946, and the birth of my sister a year later seemed to indicate that somehow a normal life was possible. It was not to be. The Soviet regime's brutality in the immediate post-war years put Dad on a constant collision course with capture, internment or worse.

So, in 1948, he escaped from Poland, knowing my mother was pregnant with their second child, and made his way into Allied-occupied Germany where he was absorbed into the U.S. Army as a former partisan. It was his ticket to North America. Nine years later, his wife and children would finally get the chance to be reunited with him in his new home – Canada.

His obedience to authority had been tested in a way most people could not possibly understand. While he always showed and preached respect for the law and, more specifically, for the foot soldiers of the law such as RCMP officers, he began to get a sense that what had happened to him at Falcon Lake and its fallout put him under a microscope, and that the so-called authorities were not treating him as a victim but as a suspect. The investigation into the UFO incident started to feel like an investigation of my Dad, not the events that he honestly and naively reported. What was black and white to him took on multiple levels of grey that he was not equipped to handle. It didn't take long for his suspicions to be aroused and encouraged by others who had more cynical agendas.

The dilemma could not be more clear. As he saw it: something bad had happened; he had been injured; the nature of the threat was unknown; it had to be reported to the proper authorities; innocents would have to be warned; he would require treatment; those authorities would have to step in, and; he could be content knowing he had done his citizen's duty. Unfortunately, life and people were not so simple. This storm he had initiated would just get worse – for him, and for his family.

Some may have turned to religion at a time like this. We were a Catholic family and regular churchgoers, although Dad had pulled away from any formal church activities. We still went on most Sundays and, of course, at Christmas and Easter. My sister sang in the choir, and since the church and elementary school were connected, I had my confirmation ceremony there.

St. John Brebeuf Church is a stunning architectural work that was completed in the year we arrived in Winnipeg. It is still an awesome church to visit. While we all drifted away from the church years later, our faith was never really abandoned. Perhaps our individual needs were satisfied in other ways. Eva left for Toronto in 1971 with a scholarship to study singing at the University of Toronto's Faculty of Music while Mark moved to Ontario in the 80s with his young family and became very active in the United Church. My mother remained a true believer until she died, and my sister and I pursued our spirituality in different ways. However, in 1967, we did not turn to the church as a family to help us through these trials. Perhaps we should have.

My father (on the left) with members of the family with whom he stayed in Saskatchewan after coming to Canada in 1949.

CHAPTER 7

Enter the Air Force

Since Dad was still in no condition to go hiking with the police, they came to him. On Thursday morning they brought a map and had Dad point out the area in which he had been prospecting on the long weekend. The RCMP was determined to go there with or without Dad, so the Royal Canadian Air Force (RCAF) became involved. Given that the RCMP really had no reference for this sort of thing, they turned to the RCAF which had developed some protocols for dealing with aerial phenomena. My brother and I were eager to find out just how this part of the investigation would proceed because of our shared interest in aviation. We would eventually be disappointed.

However, it seemed to us at the time that the bill for this investigation would continue to go up, and there didn't appear to be a limit on how much the authorities were willing to spend. It was a positive sign of sorts; at least they had not simply dismissed this out of hand as the ramblings of a crazy person.

In the afternoon, a team of RCMP officers led by Davis flew out to Falcon Lake on a RCAF helicopter, searched the area my father had indicated on the map, and came away without result. They even touched down near the Falcon Lake golf course and headed into the bush on foot, hoping to come across the site. When he was on his way into the bush on May 20, Dad had found an old saw which he placed atop a rock. He told the RCMP of this and the officers found that saw, but not the site, which would mean they were probably very close. But their expedition was a bust.

On their return to Winnipeg, Davis coordinated a repeat visit with the lead man from the RCAF, Squadron Leader Paul Bissky, who was anxious to see the site and check it for dangerous radiation (Squadron Leader was the old air force equivalent rank to Major). We had no idea what to expect when we met Bissky for the first time and, that night, my mother repeated her concerns to Dad that this was rapidly getting out of hand. On the plus side, Dad's headaches, nausea and fainting spells had subsided a little and he was able to keep down simple foods like toast, eggs and milk, but his weight continued to drop. Later, Dad confided to me that another reason he couldn't eat was because of the bad taste in his mouth – a remnant of the awful sulphur/ozone stench I had experienced mere days ago. Mom's solution was to increase his hygiene regimen. Dad now bathed daily and gave his dentures more attention. He also stopped wearing his pyjamas during the day and started to appear less like a victim and more like an outpatient.

It didn't really matter how he appeared, he was still benched by my mother and his doctors. So, when the RCMP came back to the house with Squadron Leader Bissky, the answer to whether he could accompany them to Falcon Lake was still no. Davis had checked in with Dad almost every day and had given us a break from their visits on the weekend, but it was now more than a week since May 20 and they were anxious to move the investigation along. My father made a sketch of the area describing some specific landmarks and they left with his sketches, marked maps and a plan to revisit the search tomorrow without Dad.

That evening, I listened to my parents discussing Bissky, the latest authority figure in this ever-widening investigation. Bissky was a former fighter-bomber pilot who had a brief and undistinguished tour of duty in Europe during World War II. He was a career air force man who almost had his career derailed because of a car accident in Winnipeg after the war that led to a publicized trial. The air force posted him to a remote northern base where he remained out of sight and mind for several years. On his return to Manitoba, he again made headlines, only this time he was praised for safely landing a stricken military transport aircraft and saving those aboard. He was back in the RCAF good books and was eventually promoted. Of course, I knew nothing of this at the time. All I had was a general impression of him that was delivered in Mom's usual style.

In short, she didn't like him. Unlike Davis, she considered Bissky to be cocky, a little too officious and without empathy. Besides, she said, she could not abide his smoking his fat cigars in the house. When I finally met Bissky myself, I found him to be a short fireplug of a man with a moustache, a gruff personal style, sharp laugh, and (Mom was right) an ever-present stub of a cigar which smelled bad even when it was unlit. He was not, according to my nine-year old opinion, the essence of the wartime fighter pilot. I had Rock Hudson in mind; Bissky was more like Spencer Tracy.

The mixed team of RCMP and RCAF personnel went out on May 31 and returned without success. I had a front row seat that evening as Davis and another officer described their futile attempt. They encouraged Dad to join them and, despite some angry looks from my mother, Dad agreed to go with them the next day.

All day on Thursday, I practically vibrated with anticipation. I could not concentrate at all on what we were doing at school. It was the last few weeks before summer break and the end of grade three. By the coming weekend, I would be making every effort to get underfoot and put myself squarely in the forefront of this UFO investigation. My eavesdropping had been just a taste of the happenings around our home, and I was desperate for more.

The bullying I had experienced had subsided to only a few snide comments now and again from the usual suspects. Jurek and I continued to keep in touch, and Mrs. Smith had put out the word that there would be dire consequences should anything serious happen. I considered the impending close of the school year to be the end of bad things and the beginning of good. I would have a glorious summer, and my father would be vindicated when the next story appeared in the paper that made everything right. As usual, I was dead wrong.

My Dad gives me fishing tips at a lake in Saskatchewan in the early 1960s.

CHAPTER 8

A Helicopter Ride

The tension was rising in the house. My mother had become increasingly agitated over the slightest things, so I was on my best behaviour whenever possible. For a boy my age, it was a tough challenge. I went through my school chores in a daze, hardly noticing anything that we did. I couldn't imagine how I would get through June. All I remember is zooming home every day on my bike as fast as my legs could pedal. I'm not sure what I expected to find.

Dad left early on Thursday and was likely going to be away all day. Still, the anticipation that he and the others would find the site was electric. My babbling and fussing annoyed my mother, and it was made clear to me that she did not want me in her way, jibber-jabbering about the UFO.

I played for a while, watched some TV, and found very little of any interest to listen to from my secret perch. When bedtime came, Dad had still not returned. I never heard him get home from his day at Falcon Lake.

The next morning, I was anxious to hear what had happened with the search. Mom let Dad sleep in. She said he was exhausted and still not 100 per cent, and went on a short rant about how they (the RCMP) could take him for an entire day knowing he was still sick and wear him out like that and with no result. So, I had my answer – they could not find the site.

My school day would be a disappointing blur – like having a secret that really wasn't a secret at all.

Despite being turned away at the door, newspaper reporters still managed to find something to write about. The articles that appeared in the paper now had other sources. It seemed word of the investigation had gotten out, and follow-up stories continued to show up almost daily. They treated these failures to find the site with growing scepticism and maybe there would not be the happy ending I had been expecting. Mom dutifully cut out anything she could find and began filing the stories. Years later, I would find a cardboard box filled to the brim with yellowed clippings, not only of Dad's case but others that occurred at roughly the same time.

After coming home from school, I was eager to hear from Dad what had happened. I practically burst when he told me he had been in an air force helicopter flying around the Whiteshell. He described it to me but it was Mark who told me later that it was a Hiller, a small observation helicopter with a bubble canopy and a single bench seat that could accommodate three people including the pilot. To me, it sounded like the coolest thing ever. I wanted to hear every little detail, but it didn't appear as though my father was willing to share his adventure or give me any thrilling details of his flight.

That evening, the reasons for his sour disposition became clear. It was the first time he had ever been on board a helicopter and the search ended in failure. Even when they continued on foot, Dad was disoriented and could not get his bearings. Mom scolded him for not telling the RCMP that he had never flown in a helicopter, that it was foolish for him to go up in it considering his weakened state, and that it proved nothing and resulted in less. While her voice showed concern, it was overlaid with the frustration of all of this nonsense (her word). Dad admitted that he had not told the RCMP about the helicopter ride. He also described the day's failure in detail:

how he had boarded the Hiller at a considerable distance from the Falcon Lake Motor Hotel, the start of his May 20 hike, how he had been completely lost the moment the helicopter lifted off and began criss-crossing the bush, and how he was totally disoriented when they put down and continued the search on foot.

People get lost all the time. There are many stories with unhappy endings that describe a missing person being found dead in the forest by search parties within a few hundred metres of roads and trails. Unless one experiences utter disorientation where every tree looks the same and each path leads back to where you started, it is hard to imagine.

I felt bad for him. To not have any experience with airborne searches and to be asked to spot landmarks from the air when all you see is a blur of trees and rocks must have been extremely humbling and frustrating. Many years later, when I started hiking, wilderness camping and hunting, I recall having moments where I panicked because I became momentarily distracted. Once I joined the military and learned proper map and compass technique, I thought back on my excursions and concluded that I had no idea how I managed to survive some of my youthful wilderness adventures.

My mother correctly reminded Dad that he had been in that bush before. How was it possible he could not remember where he was or where he had gone? Where was all his military training? Where was the bush craft she believed he had learned in Canada? Did he get lost because he had been injured that day? Was he still too sick? Did he need to reconsider this whole affair? Even I was beginning to feel uncomfortable as I sat on the landing listening to my Mom. I had heard that tone of voice before (and would hear it a lot more as I grew up) and I knew what was coming. Dad finally lost his temper. In his mind, the failure was his alone, and being berated for it just made it worse. For the first time since I started eavesdropping,

I crept away down the stairs, not wanting to hear how this discussion would end.

The next day was quiet in our household. Other than a phone discussion with Barry Thompson, Dad had no contact with anyone connected to the story until the RCMP checked in again. Their chat with him did nothing to lighten his mood, and there was another heated discussion between my parents that evening.

As one would expect, the RCMP were being thorough in investigating the peripheral events connected to Dad's comings and goings on the May long weekend. One set of interviews they had conducted involved whether or not he had been drinking at the Falcon Lake Motor Hotel on the Friday evening before May 20. Naturally, they interviewed the hotel's owner, the bartender on duty that night, the maid who cleaned his room, the woman at the desk, Constable Solotki, and others in Falcon Lake. They checked on his bus rides and crosschecked whatever they found.

While I didn't hear his conversation with the RCMP, I did hear the fallout when my mother brought him to task on this delicate subject. As it turned out, his side of the story that he hadn't been drinking seemed to be true. Under cross-examination from Mom, the details of what he claimed he did that Friday night and what the RCMP uncovered were almost the same. Almost.

The bartender told police that he had served my father several beers that night. However, the bar bills for that evening did not support that. He claimed he remembered Dad and the time Dad spent in the bar. Considering my father's Greyhound ticket had him riding the bus at the same time he was supposed to be at the bar, this was either a mistake or an amazing feat of being in two places at once. Did he buy liquor to take to his room? Yes. No. The maid found nothing in the room to indicate there had been any liquor of any kind. And so on...

Clearly, even if my father had consumed a few beers the night before, they would hardly have been enough to render him a hallucinating drunk the day after. And he rarely drank beer. In all the years I saw him drinking socially, beer was always his last choice if he ever chose it at all.

By the way, was it a busy night at the bar on that Friday? The bartender told the RCMP that it was extremely busy that night. Big surprise.

But, the damage had been done. This was yet another detail that would return to haunt Dad as the investigation continued. Despite the RCMP concluding that the liquor question was a non-issue, the suggestion was enough to raise my mother's ire and come back as a topic of speculation for others later in the investigation. And, Mom feared this was just something else the newspapers would write about.

On the positive side, Dad's discussion with Barry Thompson had been about the impending visit of Dr. Roy Craig from the University of Colorado, an expert on UFOs, we were told. He would bring a photographer from *Life Magazine*. This was exciting news. I loved leafing through *Life*. Now, my Dad was going to be in it. It was another case of wishful thinking. As for Dr. Craig's expertise, well...

CHAPTER 9

VIP Visitors from Colorado

In the 1950s, the United States Air Force initiated a study of UFOs called *Project Blue Book*. It was designed to gather information on all the sightings being reported (more than 12,000 once they were counted) and analyze them to determine whether they were a threat to U.S. national security. The Cold War was on, and it certainly made sense to pursue the threat angle, but what about scientific study of these reports? A few organizations received grants on behalf of *Blue Book*, including the University of Colorado. By the time Roy Craig got on board, in 1967, *Blue Book* was already in its final stages; in 1968, it would be almost wrapped up. So Craig was coming into the show a little late. There is a lot to be found on Craig's history and science methodology if one wants to look, but it's enough to say that he was a sceptic who reported to Edward Condon, a fellow scientist and famous for his work on the Manhattan Project. When the *Blue Book* project started to fade in 1968, Condon turned to Craig to write the final report. Needless to say, that report was heavily slanted towards debunking the whole UFO mythology, despite hundreds of cases that had no reasonable explanation.

When Craig showed up in Winnipeg at the beginning of June, he was mere months away from seeing *Blue Book* spiral down the drain. It almost seemed as though he dropped the gauntlet when he arrived and said, "Impress me." I remember him as being the kind of academic who is lampooned in TV shows and movies: tall, almost gaunt, with a pinched face behind horn-rimmed glasses and bushy eyebrows, and an imperious attitude that suggested he was prepared to tolerate mere mortals but not much beyond that. It didn't help matters that his visit would turn out to be unproductive.

While I went to school during the day and followed the goings on as much as possible from my secret listening post in the evenings, the only real information I could glean was that the search with what was considered to be the biggest name in UFO circles ended in failure. The photographer from *Life* took great photos of my Dad and my brother Mark in contemplative poses as they surveyed the wilderness, and shots of Craig posing like Hannibal before crossing the Alps, but there were no revealing photos of the site. It was still out there somewhere. As for a photo spread in *Life* – that was wishful thinking.

The weekend that Craig arrived had been filled with promise. I recall the positive atmosphere in the house as the principals gathered to hear Dad's story and establish their agenda for the coming expedition. When the team returned empty handed on Sunday, Dad settled into a funk that lasted for several weeks. There was simply no way to motivate him to press on regardless. He seemed to have taken this last failure as a sign that maybe Mom was right. It was time to end this.

What I could not know then was that the RCMP and the RCAF continued to follow up leads in their investigation and made several trips to Falcon Lake. Corporal Davis was able to give my father updates on what was happening, but, as far as the two investigative bodies were concerned, there was no point in spending any more time and money on this unless the site could be located. The RCMP put their investigation on hold.

Dad's weight had stabilized at around 20 or so pounds

under his average. The fact that he was now eating solid food and was not bothered as often by headaches or blackouts put him a better frame of health. But I could see he still harboured a nagging sense of failure. My mother began to focus Dad's attention on other things in an effort to buoy his spirits and help him get past the UFO experience. In a way, I suppose she believed that keeping him busy was a good way to take his mind off the events of the past few weeks. They decided that maybe it was time for Dad to return to work.

On Monday morning, we all prepared for our day. I got ready for school and Dad dressed for work. I had the sense that we were both going reluctantly.

Dad and I enjoy a hike in the woods in the fall of 1967.

CHAPTER 10

A Controversial Character Helps Find the Site

The next few weeks went by without any real movement on the UFO incident. There was some concern when a bumpy rash and swelling appeared on Dad's chest. As far as I knew, the burns had started to heal, but this was more like hives, and Dad hustled off to see his doctor. It passed in a few days.

Dad spent a lot of time on the phone and spoke with Barry Thompson on several occasions. One evening, Dad had a lengthy conversation with someone who would become a contentious figure in the story and whose involvement would muddy the relationship Dad had developed with the RCMP and the RCAF. To date, Corporal Davis had been a patient and sympathetic investigator, and Bissky, despite his off-putting personality, had appeared open minded. It all changed the day Dad agreed to meet with Gerald Hart.

My father enthusiastically described his phone conversation to my Mom and, from where I was sitting, it sounded very positive. This man, Hart, had a cabin at Falcon Lake and he was prepared to offer it to Dad as a home base from which to pursue his search for the site. It seemed like a perfectly reasonable and generous proposal and, for the first time in a while, Dad sounded very positive about the prospect. To no one's surprise, Mom was suspicious. Who was this man? What did he do? Why would he bother to help Dad? What was in it for him? I never heard the end of that conversation, although I could imagine how it would end – there would be an argument, Dad would dig in his heels and Mom would leave the discussion with her doubts unsatisfied.

On the evening of June 23, Gerald Hart came to our home to pick up Dad and take him out to Falcon Lake. He wanted my parents to call him Gerry, and that went for anyone who met him, including me. He was loud, boisterous and, when I had left the living room to take up my post on the stairs, I discovered that he was prone to peppering his conversation with four-letter words. The chat was filled with so many negative references to government agencies, the air force and the authorities that it made my head spin. Here was a stranger in our home badmouthing practically every agency that had contacted us. And, he threw in a few insults aimed at the taxman to boot. While I didn't understand many of his rants, I was surprised to discover that I found this man interesting. There was something charming about him, at least to a nine-year old. I had never met a rebel before, but based on what he was saying, rebel seemed to be the best way to describe him. Mom was not impressed. But it seemed like Hart was well connected; the cabin at Falcon Lake belonged to a friend of his who was a former crown attorney. So, when Dad and Hart left, I believed we had met a very colourful character who may have appeared like a bull in a china shop, but was sincere about helping Dad find the site thereby bringing this investigation to a speedy and positive conclusion.

After they left, Mom told Mark that she was worried that Dad had not contacted Corporal Davis about his decision to return to the bush, and she flirted with the idea of calling Davis herself to let him know. Mark didn't voice an opinion of Hart, despite the fact he was there for the whole visit, but Mom was not so shy. She called him boorish and coarse and was genuinely concerned for Dad's welfare. I never did hear if she called the RCMP or not.

On Sunday, Dad returned with the news that he and Hart had indeed found the site of the landing and that he had recovered his tape measure and some bits of his burnt shirt along with a bag of soil he scraped up from the area. He called Squadron Leader Bissky to tell him of the find and Bissky came to see Dad the very next evening.

I recall seeing Bissky arrive with an RCMP constable. It wasn't Davis. As they talked in the living room, I got the sense that their conversation was tense. Dad asked the officer how the RCMP knew of his discovery – he hadn't called them, he had called Bissky. Even at nine-years old, I could figure out that Bissky had simply informed the RCMP. They were, after all, both involved in this investigation. The discussion continued to spiral. My father, who had been respectful and co-operative with the RCMP, was now saying he was upset with the nature of the investigation – how the RCMP had inquired after his character as part of their background check. At the time, I hadn't noticed that these cross-references conducted by the police included his friends and employer. Years later, I would view them as simply part of what the police did. The results these checks produced were also positive and painted Dad in a good light. But something about how the RCMP was doing its job suddenly made Dad suspicious. It was a complete turnaround from how he had behaved with them in May.

I had to abandon my stairway in a hurry when Dad invited Bissky downstairs to see the materials he had recovered at the site. I quickly slipped into the area that had been set aside as my bedroom and busied myself with something while Dad and Bissky talked in the shop area on the other side of the divider that now separated my room from the rest of the basement.

There were only the two voices. It sounded as though the RCMP constable had been left in the living room. If I concentrated on the sounds coming from upstairs, I could hear him talking softly with my mother in the living room, while in the shop area, Dad was revealing to Bissky what he had discovered at Falcon Lake.

When they left that evening, my mother was furious. The heated discussion between them had just one theme. Mom wanted to know what Dad and this Gerry Hart character talked about while they were in Falcon Lake. And, how could he be so rude to the RCMP officer considering that they had always been very polite and patient with him? The replies Dad provided puzzled me. My father was now parroting the same colourful language that Hart had used the day he showed up at our house. Dad refused to cooperate with the police and said he would not take them to the spot until his mineral claims came through. To say the discussion between my parents was heated would be an understatement.

Bissky left the house that night with the tape and a bag of soil and forest debris with bits of Dad's burned shirt. These were turned over immediately for analysis. But Bissky left with more than that – the message Dad had delivered was clear: he had no intention of cooperating further unless it was on his terms and that Gerry Hart would be in his corner for the duration.

Who was this Gerald Hart? His absence of any respect for the government or its agencies should have been a clue that perhaps he was not the best person to assist my father. And, years later, I discovered Hart's background story when he was arrested yet again for tax evasion. At the time he first appeared on our doorstep, nobody in our family was aware of Hart's past, but the story that appeared in the paper in 1970 confirmed my mother's suspicions that Hart was the last person she wanted to see in her home. Hart had almost made a public career of fencing with the government on the subject of sales and income taxes. His unapologetic credo and the lengths to which he would defend it had become legendary. He found himself in court time and again. His arrest in 1970 led to a newspaper story with a photo in which Hart appeared wrapped in a Union Jack – a crusader for what he believed to be right and to bring to light what he called the illegal and immoral policies of the government. He even wrote a book on the subject of tax refusal (he always claimed he did not avoid paying tax, he refused to pay it). Had we known in advance that Hart had such a tempestuous past, we may not have been so willing to accept his offer of help. It proved, once again, that my mother's instincts were correct and that whatever skills my father had for sizing up people seemed to be absent. One day, following an argument with my Dad, she delivered her edict: Hart was not welcome in our home.

However, the short-term damage was already done. That my father was willing to get help and advice from Hart, a man already known to police, put Dad's relationship with the RCMP on shaky ground. It was a tenuous case to begin with; adding a character like Hart to the mix made it worse. Corporal Davis recommended that the RCMP suspend the investigation until Dad could come around. Besides, it appeared that the RCAF now had everything in hand.

We could not have known it at the time, but Davis put two and two together and guessed that Dad's change of attitude toward the police was clearly influenced by Hart. If Davis could only have been sitting with me on my stairway landing, he would have confirmed it. Not only did Dad salt his language with references to "infernal revenue" and "snivel service," his use of other creative phrases had my mother frustrated. As for the possibility that Hart would become Dad's partner in the pursuit of nickel or gold in the Whiteshell, Mom adamantly put my father on notice – there would be no further prospecting.

It was a strained environment in which I started my

summer holidays. On the one hand, they had discovered the spot, but on the other, it appeared that Dad was bent on an agenda that would alienate him from the investigators who appeared as though they were trying to help. I hoped Davis would come back and settle everything in his calm, methodical manner. I hoped discovering the site would vindicate my father. Mostly, I hoped this would end.

Thankfully, the novelty of Gerry Hart wore off in a short time. Even though Hart would try and maintain contact with our family, he was clearly aware of his status as an unwelcome guest. I remember seeing him once or twice in the years that followed, and then he simply faded away. But he left a legacy of doubt and suspicion that would dog my father for years. As for the prospecting, it's interesting to note that nothing ever came of Dad's mineral rights or his claims. If any had been in force at the time, they were allowed to expire. Dad's prospecting hobby faded, and all we had to show for it after he died was several wooden crates of rocks in the basement. I still have a few nice pieces of quartz, chipped from their mother rock by my father in a part of the Whiteshell forest not too far north of the Trans-Canada Highway.

CHAPTER 11

The Radiation Scare

Of course, nothing ended; it just heated up again. In no time, the papers picked up the story that the site had been discovered. Did my father tell them that? Did the police? I never knew how the newspapers got the information, but it seemed like our every move was being noted and published.

Dad returned to the site a week later with Barry Thompson and Bissky. They took photographs of the spot and gathered more physical evidence – mostly leaves and dirt. While Bissky was happy to have finally located the site, he was growing more suspicious about the sequence of events on that May long weekend. He was not convinced that Dad hadn't been drinking the night before. In fact, he made it his mission to try and trick Dad into admitting he had been drinking, or to find a flaw Dad's story. We never understood Bissky's obsession with the drinking angle considering the RCMP had already discounted alcohol as a factor. Perhaps there was something in Bissky's past that haunted him. We would never find out. But, we always suspected that Bissky was a sceptic and that he was pursuing this investigation as a formality. Oddly enough, his final report would show none of his personal bias. When I was able to read it years later, Bissky's conclusion was that the events of the May long weekend simply could not be explained.

There was also a constant tug-of-war with the physical evidence from the encounter. Dad's burnt brown nylon cap, his tattered and burnt undershirt, his yellow rubber-coated glove with the melted fingertips, the tape measure, his compass, the bag of dirt and debris, his original sketch of the craft – all got handed around from person to person, agency to agency. To this day, the glove and original sketch remain missing. I somehow inherited the compass from my mother after Dad died. It was broken and simply wouldn't work and, sadly, has disappeared again; it was probably the victim of a spring cleaning.

During this trading back and forth, the bag of debris and tape measure found its way into the hands of federal investigators through Bissky who had received them that evening in our basement. While various interested parties examined everything else, the dirt and tape produced the most startling results. They were radioactive. And according to the Department of Health and Welfare, there was enough cause for concern to send out their representative, a Stewart Hunt, who would arrive in Winnipeg from Ottawa in late July. The chapter we call "The Radiation Scare" was about to open. It was set in motion the day Dad found the site with Hart and collected soil, debris, bits of burnt shirt and the tape measure and put them all in the same bag. If the dirt had any radioactivity, it had contaminated everything else. The lab in Ottawa determined there was a high enough reading and the Department of Health and Welfare was prepared to seal off the area pending a closer look.

Naturally, the discovery of radiation produced several nights of discussion between my parents. My mother demanded to know if Dad had brought enough radiation into the house to contaminate the family. She was, understandably, both angry and afraid that this put everyone at risk. From where I sat, this discussion really touched a nerve – I was sleeping not 10 feet from the haversack in which my Dad had brought back those items! There was now no question that Dad would return to the site as soon as possible. The investigators had rightly convinced him that a radiation issue was a good enough reason for my father to suspend any misgivings he might have had either with or without Hart's encouragement. Mom made a solid argument. While we awaited Hunt's arrival, my mother continued to chip away at his resolve, insisting that he continue his cooperation without the presence of Hart or CAPRO. As it turned out, Barry Thompson inserted himself into the impending trip anyway and went out to Falcon Lake with the RCMP the day before.

During the last week of July, Bissky, Hunt and an Ottawa associate of his named Thompson (coincidentally, and not Barry Thompson from CAPRO) came to our house. I was pleased to see that RCMP Corporal Davis had joined them. Since wrapping up the RCMP portion of the investigation, Davis had been notably absent from our home. I think my Mom was relieved to see him as well. Perhaps he would help convince Dad that cooperation was in my father's best interests.

During the visit, Hunt checked the basement for radioactive contamination and, much to Mom's relief, found none. He was critical of how Dad had handled the items the day he found the site and even Davis was disappointed Dad had decided to bring those items back despite being told to leave the site untouched until the investigators could get there. It was a huge "I told you so" moment for my mother and, based on the atmosphere in the house, I got a feeling that Dad was being cornered. It was only a matter of time before he would give in to his frustration and dig in his heels. But, surprisingly, Dad relented and agreed to go along with them. With Mom being a gracious hostess, serving coffee and treats, and always with a smile that seemed only slightly forced, Dad gradually regained his composure and humour. From my listening perch, I could even tell through the tone of his voice and attitude towards Davis and Bissky that his outlook had improved and that this might be, in the end, a successful conclusion to the story.

For his part, Hunt was not prepared to simply take my Dad's word for it. With his associate and RCMP in tow, he made a point of investigating potential sources of radioactive materials that Dad may have sourced to hoax the whole scenario. If there was radioactivity there, where did it come from? From the search of a nearby radioactive materials dump near Falcon Lake to enquiries at Inland Cement, Hunt discovered that there was no way Dad could have got his hands on anything like radium. They even checked in with Barry Thompson and Gerry Hart (I would have liked to be a fly on the wall at Hart's business when he entertained the investigators. I'm sure that was an interesting conversation.) When it was all said and done, there was no outside source for radioactive materials and the readings of all materials proved to be below anything that could be considered dangerous.

It was now up to the group to head out to Falcon Lake and for many of the investigators to see the site for the first time, and to discover just how radioactive it was.

CHAPTER 12

Dad Writes a Book

Many years later, the radiation scare was to become a po-
tent argument for those who believed the encounter had been
extraterrestrial. From the debate about what had caused Dad's
burns to the significance of the Ottawa lab's results, the reports
of the various tests were held up as proof that this was no ordinary accident and that Dad could not have perpetrated a
hoax.

For my family's part, we were just glad to know the basement wasn't going to be glowing any time soon.

The Canadian Shield has a lot of granite, and there's an
ambient level of radiation just about everywhere. The experts
from Ottawa had brought sophisticated equipment (sophisticated for 1967) when they visited the site, and they did note a
small amount of radiation above the normal background readings. Was it enough to close the park or, at the very least, cor-
don off the area? No. But, it was an anomaly that Hunt duly
reported. He also went on to question the entire scene including how the rock had been blown clean and the resulting debris had piled up into a 15-foot diameter ring. The police and
Bissky had concluded that the site looked like it could not have
been swept clean by conventional means (like a broom), that
the area had been created by the material being somehow
blown into its circular shape. Why Hunt felt he needed to add

his two cents was curious.

It seemed to be a pattern that had developed in this investigation. Each agency came to conclusions about one piece of evidence or another and noted their findings in their reports. Then another would revisit the same finding and offer alternate opinions – like the theory that Dad had been drunk after a bender on the evening before May 20. To the RCMP, it was a non-issue. To Bissky, it was a bone of contention. To further complicate matters, Thompson and his colleagues at CAPRO proudly trumpeted the story as if it were unequivocal. Essentially, they claimed that the investigators had nothing that would disprove the sighting, therefore the sighting had to be a true close encounter with visitors from space. The downside to all of this is that most of it got published, if not in the newspaper then in APRO's newsletter, which was just another source of misinformation.

When the reporters began their assault on the house in May, Dad had been unprepared to face them and their questions. It wasn't that he was afraid; he was not completely confident of his ability to speak plainly and not be misquoted. With English as his second language, it made sense that he was reluctant. The fact that he did speak with many people about the experience became an issue. He could make mistakes while talking with his family or friends because we didn't judge him when what he was saying either didn't make sense or was poorly stated. But, he knew that there were people out there who might jump on any poor turn of phrase, and that made him nervous.

He entertained a number of visitors over the summer. Some were genuinely interested in the story as pro-UFO enthusiasts. Others were intent on learning about his medical condition and how that had been resolved. There were a few reporters with whom my Dad had long discussions. In the end, he recognized his limitations and grew tired of constantly repeating the same story over and over. Most of his visitors only wanted to hear the account of May 20. Few really cared about the resulting mayhem.

The people closest to our family offered as much support as they could. Marty and June McGregor went out of their way to maintain a normal social relationship with us, as did Halina and Mitch Bobkowski. We spent time with the Lorenc family. There were visits to each others' homes, dinners, barbecues and nice evenings. Eventually, the matter came up and it was suggested (although I'm not sure by whom) that Dad should write a book.

My father was not a writer. He had dabbled in poetry in his native Poland, but the prospect of writing a book was daunting. With much of the investigation now concluded, he had the time, but when he sat down and discussed the prospect with the family, we were not sure it was the best course of action. In the end, he decided it was not going to be a book in the conventional sense. It would be a booklet describing the events of that day and some general information about what followed. He also reasoned that the booklet would be his way of dealing with reporters in the future – when they showed up at the door, Mark could simply hand them a booklet and bid them good day – no long, exhausting interviews required. Naturally, Barry Thompson was thrilled.

Perhaps a word about APRO and CAPRO is in order. When Barry Thompson first contacted my father, Dad had been pleased to know that there was an actual organization out there that gathered and analyzed stories of UFO sightings from across North America and overseas. That the information gatherers were not scientists and that they could offer no real assistance to the people who reported the sightings didn't occur to my father. He was content to know this was an actual organization with a pretty official sounding title. What he could not know was that this was just an organization of storytellers or, more precisely, story re-tellers who printed newsletters and sent them out in hopes of somehow profiting from their service. Now that Dad had decided to put his story on paper, Thompson ramped up his involvement.

The plan was for Dad to write the manuscript in his native Polish. Thompson would then source a publisher and a translator who could re-write it in English. A man named Paul Pihichyn, a small-time publisher at Osnova Publications in Winnipeg, agreed to take on the task.

Photographs were gathered and a few of the items Dad had with him on the day of the encounter were posed for a colour cover photo. Then, Dad began to write. I recall Mark spending a good deal of time with the manuscript once Pihichyn had translated it. To this day, the grammar and spelling leave something to be desired, but the account stands up despite a few errors regarding dates and the sequence of some events. It is a testament to my father and his veracity that he never once altered or sought to enhance the story either in the book or in the many decades of re-telling that story. That it outlasted him and practically all of the investigators who descended on our home in 1967, is evidence that if it was a lie, it was one of the best lies ever told.

The small, 40-page booklet was never designed to make money. The bill came in at just under a thousand dollars when it was printed and boxed, although I never did learn how many copies were printed. Within a year or so, they were all gone. The family retained a few copies and that was that – another chapter closed. Or was it?

In later years, I discovered that CAPRO had published a story in their newsletter in 1968 which stated that my father and his family were experiencing financial hardship as a result of this case and that any interested readers of that newsletter could assist if they wanted to by sending money. However, the newsletter cautioned that in order to make sure the money reached my Dad, it should not be sent to APRO, but to a private address in Winnipeg. The address was Barry Thompson's. When the book was published, it was also promoted in the APRO newsletter as being available directly from my father for a whopping $1.00 per copy and that all money should be sent directly to my father, once again at Thompson's address.

How many copies of *My Encounter With The UFO* were sold by CAPRO? How much money was raised to assist this "needy" family in Winnipeg? We'll never know. Once the initial tale and the follow-up stories became sidebars in the APRO newsletter, Thompson disappeared from our lives. It is interesting to note that the RCMP, RCAF and Stewart Hunt all had suspicions about Thompson and his motives. My Mom also had her doubts. If we had to live through that all over again, I think we would have paid closer attention to the gut instincts of people like Corporal Davis and, especially, my mother.

My mother, me and my sister Eva in front of our Regina home in 1963.

CHAPTER 13

Of Relapses and Hypnosis

During the summer, Dad had recurring episodes of dizziness and blackouts that worried us all. While his burns had healed and the pattern of dots had all but disappeared, rashes kept showing up, and not just regular rashes but large swollen blotches that looked like mumps or hives. He saw several doctors including Oatway, but none could really help. They offered creams and salves (naturally, Mom kept track of them all), but could not diagnose the combination of dizziness and fainting spells with the appearance of the rashes. The words "allergic reaction" were tossed around again. Yes, but allergic to what?

In September, Dad was rushed to hospital. While working one day at the cement plant, he had a bout of dizziness and a burning sensation on his chest. When he went to the room they used for first aid, the pain had intensified and his neck, face and hands began to swell. The marks on his chest returned as ugly, violet blotches and he blacked out. At the Misericordia Hospital emergency room, they cut off his shirt as his wrists and arms had swollen to such a point that the shirt cuffs could not be unbuttoned. By the next day, he had recovered, the swelling had receded and the violet blotches on his chest had almost disappeared. The conclusion: an allergic reaction. Of course, we had heard that theory several times before, but why at the cement plant, why now and why did the marks

101

show up in precisely the same place as the grid pattern that had been branded onto his lower chest?

My father returned to the Falcon Lake site later that month. When he came home, he had more interesting news to share. While all of the vegetation had grown in as one would expect in the forest, the leaves on the trees surrounding the landing circle were withered, as though they had been treated with some sort of agent. Dad told us that there were some branches of nearby trees where one side of the branch held healthy, green leaves, while the leaves on the same branch but facing the landing site were crumpled and brown.

On the occasions when we had social company, discussion naturally turned to the incident – how Dad was feeling and what new information he had learned. The subject of the dying leaves came up one night. Naturally, I was supposed to be in bed, but the conversation was compelling. Had the government investigators not harvested some of the surrounding vegetation when they were at the site? Didn't they send off these samples for analysis? Just how thorough were these investigators? What we could not know was that the investigators had, in fact, gathered bags full of organic matter from the site, including leaves. What their analyses showed was not revealed to us. So, on one occasion, I recall Marty McGregor saying he would like to go with Dad and see the site for himself.

Marty was not a fan of UFOs. That is to say he was not someone who pursued the UFO stories with any real interest. He had been introduced to Dad by Mitch Bobkowski because the two had worked together in their respective professions: Mitch as an architect and Marty as a professional engineer with a specialty in surveying. So, when Marty expressed an interest, Dad was pleased to take him to the site. As it was late in the season, they agreed to go to Falcon Lake on the one-year anniversary of the event – May, 1968.

My summer was filled with all one would expect of a

OF RELAPSES AND HYPNOSIS

nine-year old. In between my activities, I continued to eaves-drop on any discussions in which UFO was mentioned. It seemed there was a lot of correspondence going on among the principal investigators including Bissky, Craig and the members of APRO/CAPRO. Dad was also handing out a lot of copies of his booklet to anyone who turned up with an interest in the case. As far as Dad was concerned, his days of lengthy discussions in which he simply repeated himself were done. That is, except for one odd encounter that I recall clearly because my Mom and brother spoke of it several times after it happened.

I never did learn who initiated this visit, and I was not present on the day it happened, but Mark's description of it was curious. And, Mark was able to provide details because he was there. Several men showed up at the house one day with the intention of interviewing Dad, then using hypnosis to put him under and have him recount the incident. Mark was the "techie" during the session, recording it all on a Sony reel-to-reel tape recorder he had purchased. We used it to record several of my sister's operatic recitals. It was a useful tool for her and her voice coach and would come in handy as she pursued her singing career. On this day, it would also serve as a useful evidence-gathering device.

The tape of that session disappeared for many years prompting many to claim that it never happened. But, after my mother died, it was discovered, like so many other things, in a box of documents and artifacts that Mom had filed away. Despite all of the cartons of seemingly useless things my mother kept over her lifetime, this one box held a few interesting tidbits that we all thought had vanished.

I recall Mark telling me what had occurred on that day. How Dad had sounded like he was talking in his sleep. He remembered Dad telling the story again, detail for detail, like he was reliving the moments. Eva was also present. She said the session finally convinced her that what Dad had been telling us was the truth. Under hypnosis, my father was reliving the moments and experiencing all of the emotional trauma associated with being burned by the craft and the nausea that followed. There were no mistakes, no embellishments. Dad told the story exactly as he had in May 1967 and exactly as he would tell it in the decades that followed until his death in 1999.

Dad looking much healthier in a photograph dated from the 1970s.

CHAPTER 14

Pieces of Silver

We celebrated a traditional Christmas in 1967. Dad's health was still a concern; he would suffer from headaches from time to time and there were bouts of fainting spells and recurring itchy rashes across his chest that came and went within days. But his weight had returned to normal and he continued to work at Inland Cement without any ill effects.

We enjoyed a mild and trouble-free spring. It was in sharp contrast to the spring of 1966 when the great Winnipeg blizzard had us snowed in for several days. Henryk Lorenc, who worked with my Dad, came home with him after their day at the cement plant, and decided that instead of just dropping Dad off, he would stay with us for the night. By then, the blizzard was causing havoc with the roads in the city and, since Henryk had a long way to drive to his home in the north end of the city, it was best that he hunker down with us and wait it out. In the morning, we woke to an Arctic landscape. Henryk's car had completely disappeared under several feet of snow that had drifted to the edge of our roof. In order to get out, he and Dad removed our back door from its hinges, took off the screen from the aluminum outer door and used a bucket to transport snow into the bathtub so it could melt and so that we could tunnel our way out of the house. It was quite a welcome to the city of Winnipeg – our first winter here and we were snowed in by a massive blizzard! It took all day to dig a path out of our home and to excavate Henryk's car, and another day for the city to plow enough of the city's streets that he could finally drive home to his family. Mom was relieved that all had ended well. If this was the worst that could happen, living in Winnipeg would turn out okay. That was 1966. She could not have known that 1967 would be worse.

In May 1968, Dad and Marty headed out to Falcon Lake. Marty took some of his surveying tools so that he and Dad could draw a more detailed diagram of the site and its location. However, that diagram was never made. Instead, they returned with something more profound that would jolt the investigation back to life in a way that no one in our home expected. Once again, the discussion between my parents was split between my Dad's need to tell someone and my Mom's insistence that we close the book on the UFO incident once and for all. Bissky was called and the wheels began to spin.

The way Marty described their Falcon Lake experience seemed, to my ears anyway, like a perfectly simple explanation. They had hiked out to the site and Dad explained the lay of the land. When discussion turned to the smear of radiation Hunt had discovered in the middle of the landing area, Marty helped Dad criss-cross the spot until they picked up the spike on their Geiger counter. Dad explained that the smear was long and narrow but quite small and, as they discussed the origins, Marty suggested that perhaps the radiation was not from what was on the surface of the rock, but what might be under it. So, with Dad's rock hammer and several hours of chipping into a crack that ran across the rock's surface, they discovered, several inches down, tiny bits of what appeared to be metal. And, judging by their generally tear-drop shape, it seemed the metal had once been molten. As they worked with the hammer and whatever small tools they had, they brought up two long pieces of metal, each about four or five inches long, that had conformed to the zig-zag gaps in the rock as though a large amount of molten material had been poured into the crack. Their Geiger counter confirmed that these pieces showed radiation. Was this the source of the earlier readings?

It was once again a matter for the authorities to determine. Dad and Marty joked that this was alien refuse. Perhaps the craft had landed to offload some waste and what they had was, basically, UFO droppings. But, despite their attempt at humour, there would be nothing to laugh at once the bits of metal made the rounds of labs and investigators.

The pieces were basically composed of silver. That's where the simplicity of it ends. Over the next year or so, there would be dozens of contradictory findings not to mention the obvious question of how the bits had got into the rock. No one was ready to suggest that the silver metal had been discharged from a UFO. The silver content was high. Once again, there was debate about whether it was abnormally higher than we could produce in a refinery, or just really pure. Then there was the chemical analysis which suggested radium, the element that had been discovered by investigators, then debunked, then re-examined, then questioned.

According to my mother, Dad had just stirred up the pot again. The discovery of the metal pieces would eventually lead to suspicions that someone close to the case had planted them. How and by whom? Fingers naturally pointed at Hart. Here was a subversive fellow who would have no problem throwing a red herring at the authorities out of pure malice. The question remained – why? And, how would my father and Marty have known to dig up the spot under which the original radiation was detected by Hunt last July? If Hart did get out to the site with the equipment he'd need to melt pure silver laced with radiation and pour the molten material into a crack in the rock, when did he do it?

Mom was suspicious of Barry Thompson throughout the

entire time he was in contact with our family. Could CAPRO benefit from having additional evidence turn up in a case that was already the most investigated incident of its kind in Canadian history? I remain doubtful.

I knew that 1968 would not bring about an end to this story. If the pieces were chapter one, then the Mayo Clinic was chapter two.

The highlight for me in 1968 was the day I got my new bicycle.

CHAPTER 15

A Visit to the Mayo Clinic

In August, Dad took a trip to Rochester, Minnesota, and checked into the Mayo Clinic. He continued to experience bouts of red bumps on his abdomen accompanied by headaches. There were fainting spells that made him worry he could harm himself or, worse, someone else. So, at the urging of family friends, he called the Mayo Clinic and registered as an outpatient. Every day for almost two weeks, Dad crossed the street from the hotel in which he had a room and underwent a battery of tests that explored each of his issues separately and together as part of his overall health. He was given a thorough psychiatric workup which, when he confided in Mom, was the most difficult part of the trip. From his point of view, dredging up details of the trauma he had experienced during the war didn't square with what he had gone through in the last year. He was an impatient patient who wanted to get to the root cause of his medical condition not the underpinnings of his psyche. As it turned out, the psychiatric report was favourable, and showed that Dad was not prone to making up a story like this for any personal gain. He was found mentally and emotionally healthy. As for the physical symptoms he had been experiencing, there were some interesting conclusions.

At the beginning of the investigation into the sighting, radiation was the bogeyman that was being blamed for many things including the burns he had suffered. Of course, that was simply untrue. The physicians at the Mayo had a theory that made sense, at least to Dad and our family and friends: he had been burned by a super-heated jet of steam or gas that ignited his shirt and undershirt and caused the burns on his chest. The question was, what compounds constituted that steam or gas? The ingredients of the chemical cocktail that burned my father were a mystery. It was no stretch to imagine that his body simply reacted to one or many of the ingredients. The initial tests showing an increased white cell count and a drop in lymphocytes backed up this possibility. Plus, he had never been allergic to anything in his life, and that only served to support this theory. As for the recurrence of the red welts on his chest and the associated nausea and headaches, it seemed logical to assume that his body was struggling to fight whatever he had been exposed to at that time. The September emergency at the cement plant was further proof – perhaps he had been exposed to one of these elements and it, by itself, triggered a reaction.

When Dad came home, the conclusions they had reached at the Mayo Clinic made perfect sense. The prognosis: that Dad's symptoms would continue to lessen until his body had successfully dealt with whatever had invaded it.

We were relieved to hear this and happy that there was hope for recovery. In the end, their prognosis was correct. Dad continued to have relapses of the spots on his chest at regular intervals for several years, but gradually the spots faded, the headaches disappeared and the fainting spells stopped. The bill for this visit was nearly $500 – a large sum in 1968. Medicare would not pay a cent, yet local doctors could not help him. It was a costly endeavour, but making the decision to go to the Mayo Clinic was one of the most responsible things Dad had done during the entire affair.

That it did not end there exasperated my mother. Eager to see the final report and not rely entirely on his own memory of the visit, Dad tried repeatedly to have the Mayo Clinic doctors send him their findings. We were all interested at the time to have the official word, and the delay only further aggravated my mother. Dad's mistake was to talk with Barry Thompson at CAPRO about the matter rather than wait patiently for the report or try another tack to get it. Thompson contacted the Mayo. When he was denied, he got APRO to check in with the clinic. Whoever replied to APRO's enquiry opened a whole new can of worms.

The Mayo representative denied ever having my father as a patient. Cries of "cover up" started echoing through the media, spurred on by CAPRO and repeated in almost every investigative circle. My mother had the bills and his Mayo Clinic ID card, not to mention his admission form and a letter from the Mayo confirming Dad's registration. It got to a point that we all believed this case had taken a sinister turn. We began to entertain the possibility that there was a cover up in the works. It just goes to show how easily the absence of an answer can lead anyone to imagine an answer, even if it's not true. It took nearly two years, but the genuine answer was embarrassingly simple. All Dad had to do was provide a personal, written and signed request for release of the records. They came right away. Scratch another bit of hysteria.

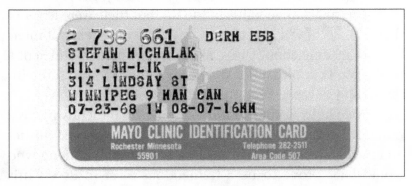

This ID card confirms that Dad was an outpatient at the Mayo Clinic.

CHAPTER 16

The Mystery Remains Unsolved

The 70s was a decade of trying to distance ourselves as much as possible from the events of 1967. Once in high school, I found that fewer people associated me with the case and, happily, I was never really bullied again. When the story did reappear as it would for years to come, we maintained a low profile in our family, and the wind generated by a media re-visit of the case never really turned into a tempest. Eventually, CAPRO and APRO lost interest. In the U.S., the *Condon Report* pretty much put a damper on the hype that had been generated in earlier decades by the tens of thousands of UFO sightings. *Project Blue Book* was closed and the populace could go back to living their normal lives – at least that's what people like Condon and Craig wanted citizens to believe. Certainly, people still reported seeing strange sights in the sky, but there were fewer of them. That's how it appeared to my family; we were not interested in reading about UFOs, although my mother still kept a pretty good clipping library, and my father showed some interest in local cases. Even that faded in time.

My family and I had formed some good friendships as a result of Dad's experience. Early in the 70s, I explored further and further from home on my new bicycle with a friend who would later prove to be a tremendous asset to us – Chris Rutkowski. As a scientist in his own right once he had finished his university education, Chris not only took a strong interest in my father's case from the day he heard about it from me, he went on to continue the investigation long after the RCMP, the RCAF, government agencies, UFO pundits and interested parties faded from view. Years after the "final" reports were submitted, Chris continued to follow cold leads and sourced forgotten documents to paint a more thorough picture of the case than any of the so-called experts of the day. He became a friend of my family, and was given our full support to do whatever he deemed fit to continue his search for answers. I suppose we thought of him as our "keeper of the flame," and consulted him every time some media agency or producer wanted to

My brother and sister, me, and my parents celebrate Christmas in 1975.

retell the story. When the attention faded, Chris kept our records in order while conducting more investigations into other sightings until he eventually earned the moniker "The UFO Guy" – the one to turn to in Winnipeg when it came to any story or event involving UFOs.

Where he differed from CAPRO and its pandering to the masses was his professional detachment. While empathetic and sympathetic, he maintained a level of scientific scepticism that gave him a level head while others around him were losing theirs. He considered all sides, and weighed conjecture against known facts, rumour against the cold truth. In a way, he earned our trust as no other person involved in Dad's story ever could.

When I finished high school, I joined the military and enjoyed my time in uniform, including overseas postings, time spent in the public affairs department and a brief stint as a staff officer with the same air cadet squadron I was in as a kid. Yes, I had followed in my brother's footsteps: Jesuit-run private high school and air cadets.

Following the military, I started working in the media. It was ironic that a member of our family should "go to the dark side," considering all we had gone through at the hands of reporters. But, it was the 80s then, and my father's story came up infrequently. My work at CKRC radio news and CKND TV finally brought me back to my first love: art and design. When I purchased my first Apple computer in 1990, I was hooked, and began my third and final career as a graphic designer. My brother moved to Ontario with his wife and two daughters, coincidentally closer to my sister who had also moved there in the 70s to continue her studies.

In 1989, we were approached by a production company in the U.S. responsible for the TV show *Unsolved Mysteries*. Of course, we called Chris to find that he, too, had been contacted by the company and that a producer would visit us to explain what they had in mind. After discussing this with my parents, and finding out what was planned, we decided that this treatment of Dad's story might be sincere enough for us to cooperate. The producer, Shannon McGinn, was very nice and seemed to be genuinely interested in telling a well-balanced story that would have no embellishment. It was refreshing to hear that she was interested in recounting the incident and not exploiting the story for its wow factor. They would, of course, stage a re-enactment and use CGI to replicate the UFO, and include on-camera interviews with Dad, Chris and myself. They

I marched in my brother's footsteps in the air cadets and got to fly in a number of different aircraft including this L-19 Bird Dog.

would also add clips of Ed Barker, who worked at the Planetarium in Winnipeg, and had been a very interested party when the story broke in 1967. The unique aspect of this project was that it would be shot in Deadwood, South Dakota.

Anyone who has ever visited the Canadian Shield at Whiteshell Provincial Park, or any points further east towards Kenora, knows what the terrain looks like. There is an abundance of conifers and rock – lots of rock – and very little change in elevation (although the land does rise as one travels east of Winnipeg). Shooting the re-enactment in the rolling hills of South Dakota produced an interesting opening shot in the *Unsolved Mysteries* episode. When Dad saw the finished segment, he was the first to notice the anomalies in the scene showing the actor who portrayed him cresting a hill surrounded by the kind of vegetation that grows in South Dakota, not Manitoba. With the hills in the background, it may as well have been the opening bit from the *Sound of Music*. But, we were all ready to forgive this slight inaccuracy once we watched the rest of the segment which first appeared in November, 1992.

Shannon lived up to her promise. The piece was well done – probably the best review of the case ever done by any media outlet, and the best re-enactment of the events according to Dad. *Unsolved Mysteries* could also be forgiven for showing a very fanciful interior of the UFO because, quite frankly, Dad was not much help in describing what he saw when he poked his head inside the opened portal of the craft. They did the best they could for that shot.

The interviews were conducted in a house the company had rented for the shoot. It was supposed to represent our house and failed utterly, but that was a small matter. All interviewees were parked on a chair in the middle of the living room and were, in turn, interviewed by an off-camera producer who was also very friendly, sensitive and attentive, stopping the interviews when he thought Dad might like a pause. As someone who worked in television, I was familiar with the pro-cess and spent some time observing the crew and how they worked. I was not surprised to see that they were mostly going through the motions, working as if by rote, following instruc-tions and showing little interest in what was being said. I sup-

Dad is interviewed on the location set of *Unsolved Mysteries*.

pose it was normal that they should be somewhat jaded, having taped endless interviews with people who had bizarre stories to tell. I guess not all unsolved mysteries are compelling.

As I watched the process, there was a lull in Dad's interview while the crew repositioned lights and cameras, and changed batteries. The interviewer continued to make small talk with Dad while they sat, and asked, "Well, I guess this has to be the most difficult and remarkable thing that has ever happened in your life." Dad responded, "Oh, no." Taken aback, the producer asked him to explain.

For the next 20 minutes or so, Dad recounted his war experiences, his internment in Gross-Rosen concentration camp, and the years after the war when he escaped from Poland and joined the U.S. Army occupying Germany. Part of his job with the allied forces was to act as a translator and go to several concentration camps that were being dismantled in Eastern Ger-

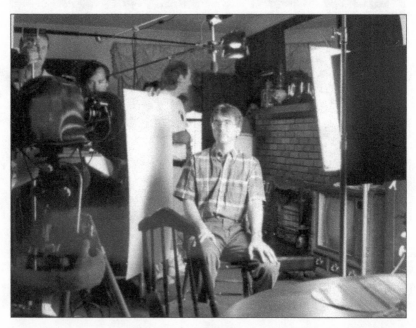

Chris Rutkowski on the hot seat during the shooting of *Unsolved Mysteries*.

many. The horrors he saw there were still vivid more than 40 years later. As he spoke, I noticed that the crew had stopped working and listened to my father without moving and in complete silence – the lights and cameras turned off. When Dad stopped, the producer, visibly shaken by what he'd heard, decided it was time to break for lunch.

The entire team's attitude toward Dad and his UFO story changed immediately. The crew were now interested in what he had to say and treated him with a deference that showed a real measure of respect. During lunch and after the production wrapped, I was approached by Shannon and the interviewer who both told me that my father was a remarkable man. I chatted with some of the crew who admitted to me that their job of criss-crossing the country looking for unsolved mysteries often left them questioning the truth of the stories and the sincerity of the subjects. On this day, they had been convinced

Christmas, 1988. As always, we dressed up for family occasions.

that here was a truthful, sincere man who had already lived through many hardships. Why would he bring something like this on himself and his family if it weren't the truth?

In the years that followed, Dad's health deteriorated. He became diabetic and had heart issues that dogged him until he died in 1999. In all those 32 years, he lived with the memory of what he saw that day in 1967 and never altered the story, never embellished it to make it look any better or worse, never felt that he needed people to believe him (or cared if they did not), never sought to become an evangelist for the UFO cause, and believed that it was simply fate that had put him in that spot on May 20. He was bitter that others might have capitalized on the account which, to him, had been a simple matter of reporting what he had encountered and having the authorities make it right. Naturally, the very nature of the report was grist for the media mill and would, eventually, add more fuel to the hysteria that was being generated by UFO encounters.

For my part, I had always believed that what he said was the truth and that any other explanation for the events and their brutal effects on his health and the well being of his family absolutely disregarded his character. He was not afraid that day, though he was not a fearless man. He had seen and done enough in his life to fill a filing cabinet with the post-traumatic effects of fear. His fear only came once he realized he had been hurt and what that might do to him, to his family and to others.

He was curious. That was Dad to a tee. In the *Unsolved Mysteries* segment, he said his reaction to seeing the craft for the first time was, "What the hell is that?" That was the man I grew up with. Whenever I encountered anything I did not understand, Dad taught me to approach with curiosity, not fear. A man who has stared death in the face and has seen the aftereffects of genocide would not run in fear from the unknown, even if it took the form of a UFO. That he approached the craft to see if there was anything he could do to help shows that the events that day became fearful only after he was injured. He even cautioned others in his booklet not to get too close should they ever have the same experience. It made perfect sense that the closing sentence of his personal account should serve as a warning.

For my part, I believe that taking the measure of a man and learning what makes him tick serve a greater purpose in understanding him when the worst happens and he faces danger or the unknown, or is called upon to recount any experience that others might find impossible to believe.

I have spent the last 50 years trying to live up to that creed.

Me, Eva and Mark in a photo dated from the late 1990s.

PART 4

The Falcon Lake Case:
A Review

By Chris Rutkowski

INTRODUCTION

Throughout the UFO literature, there are many stories of alleged physiological effects or injuries associated with UFO encounters. There are several published reviews of these cases, including Aggen (1969), Crain (1971), Tokarz (1978) and the definitive summary by McCampbell (1987). In addition, reviews of close-encounter cases often include details of medical reactions and effects associated with UFO experiences. The most well-publicized and investigated physiological-effect case in recent ufological history was the Cash-Landrum encounter, in which two women said they were confronted by a diamond-shaped object and suffered various injuries as a result (Schuessler 1984).

One of the most intriguing cases of serious injury attributed to a UFO experience occurred on May 20, 1967, approximately 75 kilometers north of the American border in the rocky periphery of the great Canadian Shield. Stefan Michalak returned home from a prospecting expedition with serious ill effects that he claimed were a result of an extraordinary UFO encounter near Falcon Lake, Manitoba, Canada (Rutkowski 1981a).

For the next two years, Michalak was examined by more than one dozen physicians in the United States and Canada. Site investigations were made by members of the RCMP, RCAF, government officials and several civilians. The number of government departments and officials who were involved in this case is staggering. In the ground party that travelled with Michalak to the site were representatives of: the RCAF (Royal Canadian Air Force) Training Command

Headquarters; CFB (Canadian Forces Base) Winnipeg; RCMP CID (Criminal Investigations Division); the federal Department of Health and Welfare; and the Manitoba provincial Department of Health and Welfare. In addition, the University of Colorado Condon Committee (commissioned by the United States Air Force to study UFO reports) investigated, *Life Magazine* reporters came to Manitoba, and two connected but separate civilian groups, APRO (Aerial Phenomena Research Organization) and CAPRO (Canadian APRO), became involved. Furthermore, the provincial Department of Mines and Natural Resources took an interest, as did the Whiteshell Nuclear Research Establishment (WNRE), the Manitoba Cancer Institute, the Mayo Clinic, and a host of other medical establishments.

The scope of this intense investigation cannot be understated. The Falcon Lake case may well be one of the most intensely investigated and well-documented on record. The case presents a number of elements of particular interest to researchers:

- Michalak's burns and other physiological effects;
- The large number of investigators involved and witnesses for Michalak's character;
- The ground traces and radioactivity found at the site; and
- Mysterious metal fragments found at the site.

PHYSIOLOGICAL EFFECTS

When asked by an examining doctor how he had been injured, Michalak originally said he had been "hit by exhaust coming out of an aeroplane." He was having difficulty putting into words what he had experienced, and his own grasp of English was a barrier to being understood. He was very tired and wanted to go home. He was given a sedative and went home, where he took a bath to cleanse his wounds then went to bed. (Michalak 1967: 23) The next morning, Michalak was still in some pain and his family noted he had extremely bad body odour and halitosis. He could not hold any food down, but he was not hungry anyway. He said that according to the bathroom scale he had lost six pounds during the previous two days, and he became concerned.

It was not until that evening that his own physician, Dr. R. D. Oatway, examined Michalak and was told the saucer story. Michalak noted: "He looked at me with what one may call a professional discretion." (Michalak 1967: 24) Oatway's detailed report, prepared for APRO consultant Dr. Horace Dudley, describes Michalak's physical condition at that time:

"He complained of band-like headache, hot forehead, anorexia and nausea, feeling of blacking out. On examination, he appeared rather depressed, dazed, apathetic, but rational and coherent. There was singeing of the hair on the forehead at the hairline and over the lower sternal and upper abdominal region. Over the upper abdomen, in the mid-portion and especially to the left of the midline, there were numerous reddish,

```
    PCB129VV   PVA241HA103    UU      MAY 23 20  25 '67
PP RCCVC
R RCVPT 116 23/1836Z
P 231830Z MAY 67                                O.P.I.  cfoc
FM RCC WINNIPEG   PRIORITY
TO CANFORCEHED                         Our OPS-4/21
BT                                     3-3200 may requests
UNCLAS A0662                           Contravention to investigate
FOR CFOC. UFO REPORT                   same.
A 1700E 20 MAY 67
B CLOUDY SKY
C MR S MICHALAK, 14 LINDSAY ST WINNIPEG 9 MANITOBA. PHONE
489-3162
D FALCON LAKE MANITOBA. 4941N 9515W
E NIL
F TWO OBJECTS ON GROUND APPROX 35 TO 40 FEET IN DIAMETER, EIGHT
FEET HIGH, SAUCER SHAPED, COLOUR OF UNPOLISHED STEEL ON GROUND
AND CHANGING TO HEATED METAL COLOUR ON DEPARTURE
G EXCESS OF ONE HALF HOUR
H MR MICHALAK OBSERVED THE TWO UFOS FROM A SHORT DISTANCE FOR ONE
HALF HOUR AND OBSERVED ONE DEPART VERTICALLY THEN HEAD SOUTH.
HE WENT UP TO THE REMAINING ONE, OBSERVING AN OPEN DOOR WITH A
VIOLET LIGHT PREVENTING HIM FROM SEEING INSIDE. AS HE APPROACHED

PAGE 2 RCWPC 116 UNCLAS
HE COULD HEAR A WHIRRING SOUND AND INDISTINGUISHABLE VOICES
FROM WITHIN. UPON TOUCHING THE OBJECT WITH HIS GLOVED LEFT HAND
HIS GLOVE BURNED, THE DOOR CLOSED AND THE OBJECT STARTED ROTATING
COUNTER-CLOCKWISE THEN DEPARTED VERTICALLY ALSO HEADING SOUTH.
HIS SHIRT WAS BURNED FROM THE EXHAUST PANELS ON THE OUTER EDGE
AND HE REQUIRED MEDICAL TREATMENT FOR BURNS ON HIS STOMACH. HE
HAS LOST TWELVE POUNDS SINCE AS HE HAS BEEN UNABLE TO EAT.
WHILE HE WAS APPROACHING HE COULD SMELL WHAT HE RELATES TO AS AN
ELECTRICAL FIRE. THE NOISE INCREASED IN PITCH TO A HIGH WHINE ON
TAKE OFF
BT
13" 200                                    (1)
```

The first official document concerning Michalak's UFO report. This is a teletype sent by CFB Winnipeg to Canadian Forces Headquarters in Ottawa, on May 23, 1967.

slightly irregular, oval-shaped, slightly raised lesions, arranged with their long axes mainly in a transverse direction. These lesions seemed to be consistent with a first-degree burn. As I recall they were painful and tender but not severely. I also observed the burnt undershirt which had holes with charred (or blackened) edges corresponding to the site of the burn."
(Oatway 1968)

Oatway examined the burns and prescribed antinausea tablets and codeine painkillers. Later, he referred Michalak to a dermatologist who gave him some antibacterial skin cleanser for the burns. During the next two weeks, Michalak's condition improved gradually. He kept a diary of his health during this time. He noted that his weight decreased from 180 lbs. before his UFO encounter to a low of 158 lbs. on May 27, one week later.

Unfortunately, since Michalak had not seen his personal physician for more than a year before his UFO encounter, there was no official record of his pre-encounter weight. During this time, he also experienced several fainting spells, which he had never had before in his life. He continued to vomit occasionally, but his appetite slowly returned to normal. As a result of prompting by civilian UFO investigators, Michalak went to a radiologist on May 23., but no evidence of radiation trauma was found.

On May 30, Michalak was taken by a UFO investigator to the Whiteshell Nuclear Research Establishment, where he was given a whole-body count. Again, nothing above normal background readings was found. During the period immediately following his encounter, Michalak had a slight drop in blood lymphocyte count, from 25 per cent to 16 per cent.

As noted by one investigator, the specific values and corresponding times were:

May 24, 1967 16%
May 30, 1967 21%
January 15, 1968 31% (Cannon 1970)

After four weeks, the white-cell count was reportedly back to a normal level. During this time the platelet counts were consistently normal. If Michalak had been affected by radiation, as some have suggested, the counts would have varied more significantly. Brian Cannon, a founder of CAPRO, reported to that group's membership that the heal-

$\underline{\text{M E M O R A N D U M}}$

Westwin, Man,
26 May 67

S/L P Bissky
SSO AIROPS/TC

Re: Telephone Communication
Mr. Steve Mychalak

1.   I have at your request contacted the physician who examined the above named, Saturday evening 20 May at Misericordia General Hospital Winnipeg, following Mr. Mychalak's reported exposure to an UFO.

2.   At the time of examination the physician was unaware of the circumstances surrounding Mr. Mychalak's burns.

3.   At examination the physician found an area of first degree burns over the upper abdomen, covering an area of 7-8 inches and consisting of several round and irregular shaped burns the size of a silver dollar or less. These were a dull red in color, the hair over the lower chest was singed as was the hair on the forehead with some questionable redness of the right cheek and temple.

4.   Subsequently Mr. Mychalak complained of feeling ill and his clothes and blood were checked for radiation and found to be negative.

5.   As of this date Mr. Mychalak is reported to be feeling better.

6.   If anything further is descovered the physician has offered to call me.

SGD

(D J SCOTT) SgLCDR
Deputy Base Surgeon
542

Memo from D.J. Scott, Base Surgeon of CFB Winnipeg, to P. Bissky, dated May 26, 1967, detailing Michalak's injuries as recorded by the ER doctor at the Misericordia Hospital on the night of May 20, 1967, in Winnipeg.

ing of Michalak's burns was "a characteristic trait of radiation burns." (Cannon 1968) One hematologist's report, however, indicated "no abnormal physical findings," although Michalak had "some atypical lymphoid cells in the marrow plus a moderate increase in the number of plasma cells." (Oatway 1968) These minor variations do not support some published accounts that claim Michalak had impurities in his blood (Naud 1978).

But Dr. Horace Dudley, a radiologist and APRO advisor at the University of Southern Mississippi, observed that Michalak's

> "... nausea and vomiting followed by diarrhea and loss of weight is a classical picture of severe whole body [exposure to] radiation with x- or gamma rays. I would guess that Mr. Michalak received on the order of 100-200 roentgens. It is very fortunate that this dose of radiation only lasted a very short time or he would certainly have received a lethal dose."
> (Lorenzen and Lorenzen 1968: 40-41)

Others did not believe that symptoms of radiation poisoning were present, and the issue has never been fully resolved (Michalak 1967: 27-28; Rutkowski 1981b).

Michalak's skin problems also had different interpretations. His upper chest, having been diagnosed as thermally burned, healed fairly rapidly. His abdomen, where the grid pattern appeared, went through periods of fading and recurrence. It had been suggested that these welts were radiation burns.

Michalak also had a rash that broke out on his upper torso. One investigator said this was due to insect bites, and this is supported by the fact that investigators were indeed bitten by large numbers of black flies at the site. However, it does appear that Michalak had more than just a simple patch of bites. Medical records noted he had skin infections that were "hive-like areas with impetiginous centers." (Oatway 1968) In another report, he had "generalized urticaria." (Oat-

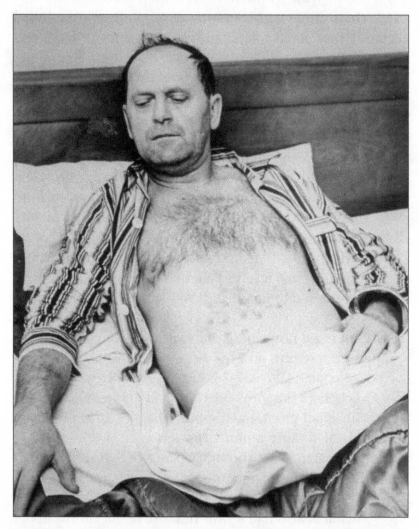

Michalak at home in bed, shortly after the incident. The "silver dollar" burns are clearly visible on his abdomen, arranged in a regular pattern. The hair on his upper chest is visibly charred as well, consistent with his open shirt collar.

way 1967). Along with the recurrence of the rash (urticaria), Michalak reported feeling weak, dizzy and nauseous, and he experienced numbness and swelling in his joints (Michalak 1967: 35-36).

It is possible that Michalak had an allergic reaction to something in the environment. On September 21, 1967, four months after his UFO experience, Michalak was at work when he became very ill. He felt a burning sensation on his chest and neck, his throat constricted and he became very flushed ("turned violet"). His hands swelled "like a balloon," he became dizzy, then fainted (Michalak 1967: 35). Upon examination, doctors concluded that Michalak had had an allergic reaction of some sort. However, considering that he had never had such reactions before his encounter, one might wonder what had triggered the episodes.

Michalak gradually recovered from his injuries and stopped having his recurring allergic reactions. Until his death, however, the strange array of burn scars could be still felt underneath the skin of his lower abdomen.

THE MAYO CLINIC

In August 1968, Michalak went to the Mayo Clinic in Rochester, Minnesota. The purpose of his visit was to undergo tests in order to determine exactly what was ailing him, since the doctors in Winnipeg appeared to be unhelpful. It is worthy to note that Michalak paid for the Mayo tests entirely on his own, as Canadian medical insurance would not cover such a trip. He travelled south and stayed for two weeks at a motel near the hospital, walking across each day and entering as an outpatient. He reported that he was given a thorough physical and psychological examination by various doctors, then sent home.

Michalak waited for several weeks, but received no word on his results. He complained to his own doctor and told CAPRO representatives of the lack of results. CAPRO investigators appealed to APRO for help. Eventually, ufologist John Keel intervened and as a result, Dr. Berthold Schwarz, a

sion. His appetite is good and he sleeps fairly well. He admits to no phobias, does not expect to see the apparition again, has no fears about his experience except regarding the danger his blackouts might cause. He is a pleasant, warm man capable of humor. Initially he is somewhat defensive but he warmed during the lengthy interview and expressed his opinions freely and easily. He carries a briefcase, on request willingly demonstrated his lesions, and spontaneously showed the pieces of metal from the alleged vehicle which, he says are of unknown type. I found no evidence of delusions, hallucinations. He impresses me as being a compulsive man who probably has considerable repressed anger and depression but who has functioned adequately and adapted well to a new environment. The MMPI was not extraordinary. Despite the fact that his lesions have been diagnosed as obviously factitial, I can find no overt evidence of significant mental or emotional illness. To do so might require further interviews and corroboration of data from other sources.

Excerpt from the report on Michalak's mental health by the examining psychiatrist at the Mayo Clinic in Rochester, Minnesota. He noted: "I found no evidence of delusions, hallucinations... I can find no overt evidence of significant mental or emotional illness." In other words, despite what some people may think about UFO witnesses being deluded, the Mayo Clinic psychiatrist found Michalak to be well-adjusted and rational.

psychiatrist and ufologist, assisted by sending a letter of inquiry to the Mayo Clinic, asking about the medical reports. In reply, he was sent what has been referred to as the "letter of denial." Dated (perhaps significantly) April 1, 1969, the letter bluntly stated:

> "I have checked through our registration desk and I find that we have never had a patient by that name registered at the Mayo Clinic. If he had been a patient I suspect that I would not have been able to send you information without a release from him, state laws being what they are, but I can tell you we don't know anything about him."
> (Barry 1969)

This immediately spurred shouts of "cover-up!" from some individuals who learned of the letter, as this appeared to be a deliberate attempt to mislead the investigation. However, Schwarz tried again, with a different tactic; he asked Michalak to sign a simple medical records release form and forwarded that to the Mayo Clinic in January 1970. The reports came immediately.

Michalak had been found to be in good health but with neurodermatitis and simple syncope (fainting spells due to sudden cerebral blood pressure losses). The syncope was suggested as having to do with hyperventilation or impaired cardiac output (Rovelstad 1970). This is interesting, as Michalak indeed had heart problems later in his life. Furthermore, the Mayo Clinic report described Michalak's physiological problems in more detail:

> "Since May, 1967, he has had repeated clearing-up and recrudescence of the erythematous and pruritic lesions on his chest and legs. Sometimes these occurred at in-

tervals of approximately 112 days, but this has not been consistent. Since January, 1968, reoccurrences have been more frequent but the symptoms were briefer in duration. Generally, the chest lesions appear as minute points or 'grains,' enlarge progressively to the size of a quarter or a half dollar, and are very pruritic ... The time between initial appearance and disappearance has ranged from a few days to several weeks. Various medications have not been helpful."
(Mayo Clinic 1968: 1)

His condition was viewed as being quite serious, especially given the following information:

"Mr. Mechallack's [sic] main reason for coming to the Mayo Clinic now is because of headaches and 'blackout spells' which have attended the other symptoms since he was severely ill in January, 1968. Headaches are mainly bitemporal, steady, and excruciating. Skin problems occur at the same time. Blackout spells are not sudden but cannot be predicted accurately enough to permit him to drive during symptomatic periods (he is fearful of hurting himself and/or others). Gradually, his eyesight begins to dim until everything goes black. He has time to sit down but is ... unconscious for a few minutes or more. Allegedly, his wife has viewed him during these spells and he recounts no symptoms suggestive of seizures. He declares that he is unable to hear during the spells."
(Mayo Clinic 1968: 1)

CHARACTER OF THE WITNESS

At the time of the incident, Stefan Michalak was an employee of an industrial facility in Winnipeg; he was an industrial mechanic, with knowledge of automotive machinery, welding, and metalwork. With regard to Michalak's mental state, an examining psychiatrist at the Mayo Clinic noted:

"I found no evidence of dreams [or] hallucinations ... The MMPI [a tool used by psychiatrists to evaluate the mental health of a patient] was not extraordinary ... I can find no overt evidence of significant mental or emotional illness"
(Mayo Clinic 1968: 2)

Michalak had never before reported observing anything like the UFO he encountered in 1967. During World War II, he had been an intelligence officer and was very familiar with the appearance and behaviour of military vehicles.

In the RCAF report on the incident, much was made of Michalak's association with a man named Gerald Hart (RCAF 1967a). Hart was described by the RCMP as a "subversive" individual, so when Michalak told them that Hart had assisted him in his quest for the site of his encounter, officials became suspicious. (Among other eccentricities, Hart refused to pay income tax and in fact wrote a popular book on how to avoid paying the government anything.)

Furthermore, the actions of civilian UFO investigators were cause for concern in the minds of officials. In particular,

Barry Thompson, described by a former CAPRO member as a "liaison between CAPRO and APRO," was:

"... a constant companion of Mr. Michalak and he appeared to be the spokesman for Mr. Michalak during some of the interviews. Both the investigating officer and Professor Craig [of the Condon Committee] agreed there appeared to be monetary gain intentions associated with this relationship."
(RCAF 1967a: 4)

However, there was never any "monetary gain" from the incident. Michalak's own narrative account was privately published in late 1967. His manuscript, written in Polish, was

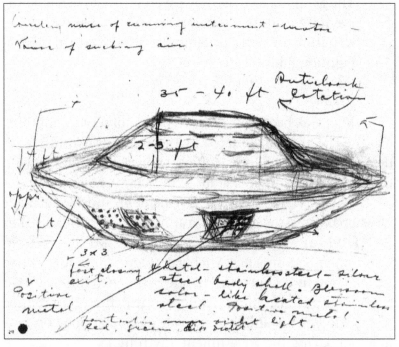

The sketch by Michalak of the object he eventually approached, indicating the location of the "exhaust vents" and the door from which shone bright purple lights.

translated and printed as a 40-page booklet that quickly sold out. Michalak saw little of the money recovered after publication costs, and was bitter that "others have made money from my experience, but not me" (Michalak 1980). Actually, because of the small run and limited circulation, the publisher likely lost money.

Squadron Leader Paul Bissky of the Royal Canadian Air Force was the investigating military officer on the case. His reports to Canadian Forces Headquarters are remarkable in their detail and candid comments about his investigations. But complicating his reports is the fact that Bissky was a devout sceptic, and told researchers he "didn't believe in that stuff [UFOs]" (Bissky 1980). How much his personal opinions may have influenced his reports is not known.

That Bissky thought Michalak was a liar is an understatement. At one point during his investigation, he bluntly asked Michalak if he had been drinking on the day of the experience. He believed that Michalak was hallucinating because of some alcoholic stupor. Bissky appeared sure that alcohol was somehow involved with the case, and he cleverly manipulated Michalak into proving he was not a teetotaler. In his first report, Bissky noted:

> "Although the authenticity of Mr. Michalak's report had not been questioned up to the second search, he had appeared genuinely sincere and his story was convincing to those who heard it for the first time, some doubts arose during the last search... Mr. Michalak had staunchly denied having consumed alcoholic beverages at any time while at Falcon Lake. Yet a reliable witness at Falcon Lake advised that he personally had served Mr. Michalak 4 or 5 bottles of beer the night prior to the trip into the bush."
> (RCAF 1967a: 2)

The "reliable witness" was a bartender, and Bissky did not state how his source's own reliability had been established. Bissky seemed to want to prove there was at least one inconsistency or lie in Michalak's testimony, and the issue of alcohol consumption seemed to be a choice target. (In retrospect, even if Michalak admitted drinking several beers, there would still remain the problem of the other physical and physiological evidence; Michalak's drinking probably had no bearing on the case itself.)

In his later report, Bissky noted several "discrepancies" in Michalak's story, including this following detailed passage that gives us some insight into Bissky's RCAF investigation:

"... it was proven that Mr. Michalak does consume alcoholic beverages, in fact to some considerable extent. After coming out from the alleged site, Mr. Michalak was purposely taken to the same bar where he had consumed the five beers the night prior to his initial encounter on the 20 May 67. Although he declined the offer of beer (it could not be determined whether this was done because he did not like beer or not), he did accept the offer of several rye 'Presbyterians' (rye and half water/ginger ale mix), in fact he even went so far as to purchase a round of drinks for the group. He appeared to hold his alcohol reasonably well, although it was noticed that he did loosen up after the third drink and become quite gay, telling numerous stories. When questioned about the vast discrepancy in direction the object departed, he just shrugged his shoulders and laughed it off. When last seen, he was in a jovial mood, remaining at the bar, presumably to await the arrival of his two assistants from Winnipeg. Hence it is very possible that Mr. Michalak may have had a private party on his own the night of 19 May, which in turn

could have caused hallucinations the following day."
(RCAF 1967b: 4)

In effect, Bissky attempted to get Michalak drunk and get him to let his guard down, to prove his belief that Michalak had hoaxed the whole affair. Bissky was convinced that Michalak had drunk heavily the night before his alleged experience, causing him to have imagined or made up the entire UFO encounter ten to twelve hours later.

Bissky later described an alternative theory: Michalak had been drinking and burned himself on a hot barbecue grill. Support for this idea came from another of Bissky's unnamed but "reliable sources," in this case a woman who was awakened by Michalak pounding on her cabin door at 2:00 a.m. Unfortunately, Bissky said that the woman was at Falcon Lake for a "tryst" and could not come forward publicly. It is interesting that this explanation was never mentioned in any official report, and has no other evidence to support it (Bissky 1980). Despite all of his attempts to find flaws in Michalak's story, Bissky was forced to concede that:

> "... there are certain facts, such as Mr. Michalak's illness and burns and the very evident circle remaining at the site, which are unexplainable."
> (RCAF 1967b: 5)

Even under the intense scrutiny of biased military investigators, the case appeared sound.

RADIATION

On June 23, 1967, Michalak travelled to Falcon Lake with Gerald Hart. Hart had offered to help in the search, and told Michalak he visited the area frequently on his own. Michalak took him up on his offer.

> "He not only took me there but helped me in the search. I looked throughout the woods checking rocks I had seen before, examining chips I had made in the stone and finally, after six hours, we came upon the spot."
> (Michalak 1967: 31)

They found a ring of debris, thought to have been made when the object lifted off. In addition, they found bits of Michalak's shirt and his tape measure that he had left behind. When they returned to Winnipeg, they informed the RCAF of their findings.

On July 2, RCMP, RCAF and CAPRO investigators accompanied Michalak to the site, gathering samples and taking photographs. The RCMP analyses of the samples showed significantly high radiation readings. On their recommendation, consideration was given to cordoning off the area due to a possible health hazard. This was noted in an *Incident Report* from an inspector with the RCMP Crime Laboratory in Ottawa, the result of tests on some samples sent by the RCMP to the Department of National Health and Welfare. They found:

"... a radiation value of .3 microcuries in the soil sample... the radiation is from a radium source and is a possible serious health hazard." (RCMP 1967)

Samples taken from the site by Michalak and Hart were eventually tested by the Radiation Protection Division of the Canadian Department of National Health and Welfare. They examined samples of "soil, burned shirt and steel tape for possible radioactive contamination." The initial gamma analysis showed significant levels of "Ra 226 or its equivalent."

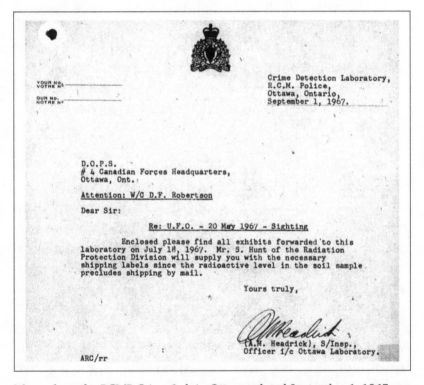

Memo from the RCMP Crime Lab in Ottawa, dated September 1, 1967, accompanying the samples and other items tested for radiation. Despite the fact that radiation levels were not high enough to be considered by Provincial experts as hazardous to the public, the levels were considered by the RCMP too high to send through the mail.

In a report prepared by Stewart Hunt for A. K. Das-Gupta, the head of the Safety Assessment and Control Section of the Division, details of the radioactivity assessment were described. Hunt outlined very clearly and cautiously the reasons his Division was involved:

"The task of assessing the radiation hazard to the general public and the landing site did not initially indicate that it would be necessary for the Division to involve itself in the RCMP and DND investigation. However, it became obvious ... that collection and co-ordination of all background information was essential due to the following:
a. The apparent lack of cooperation by the principals toward the military and police.
b. The exact location of the sighting had not been established at the time of the Division's initial involvement."
(Hunt 1967: 1)

Hunt flew to Winnipeg and met with various other officials on July 26, 1967. They had a brainstorming session, during which they arrived at a complicated plan of action that included a thorough investigation of the site, analyses of the physical effects and a detailed background check not only of the principal witness but also of the civilian investigators.

As part of their investigation, the team travelled to East Braintree, Manitoba, near the Whiteshell, where hazardous waste from the Manitoba Cancer Institute was buried. The reason for this was the suggestion that someone had "seeded" the landing site with commercially produced radium. If it had not come from a radium watch dial, they reasoned that it must have come from a nuclear waste disposal site. Again, the seriousness with which the case was regarded is evident. Tampering with a nuclear waste disposal site is a very grave matter. No indication of tampering was found, however.

The team also visited Michalak's place of employment to see if it used radium in any of its products. They then visited Michalak at his home to check for radiation in the samples he had in his basement. Hunt noted:

27 July 1967, 1200 hrs. – Met S/L Bissky, F/O Smith, Cpls. Shepard and Reed, all of the R.C.A.F., Cpl. Davis and Constable Zacharias of the R.C.M.P., and Mr. Michalak at the Falcon Lake Provincial Park entrance. After lunch, the above mentioned plus Thompson and Hunt set out for the U.F.O. landing site. This involved crossing to the north side of Hwy. No. 1 and following the route as indicated on the attached map. The entire expedition took about 45 minutes to reach its destination. The site was confirmed as being the correct site by Constable Zacharias who had been taken to it by Mr. B. Thompson of the Winnipeg Airborne Phenomena Research Organization the night before. The landing area of the U.F.O. was recognizable from the photographs taken by Life Magazine, the origin of the circular outline of vegetation in the writer's opinion is debateable. A thorough survey of the landing area was carried out, using a Tracerlab SU1A, Admiral Radiac 5016, and a Civil Defence CDV 700 survey meter. One small area was found to be contaminated. This was located across the crown of the rock. There was a smear of contamination about 0.5 x 8.0 inches on one side of the crack. There was also some lichen and ground vegetation contaminated just beyond the smear. The whole contaminated area was no larger than 100 square inches. All water run off areas were checked for possible contamination, but nothing was found. Samples of the contaminated rock and lichen were taken for further analysis. Photographs of the are were taken by Cpls. Shephard and Davis and Mr. Thompson. Since there was no serious health hazard involved due to the remoteness of the area and also due to the fact that the majority of the contamination was taken for samples, no further precautions were felt necessary at the U.F.O. site. Prior to returning to Winnipeg, it was decided that Messrs Hunt and Thompson would try and establish the source of the radioactivity by paying a visit to Mr. B. Thompson.

Conclusions

The undersigned does not intend to prove one way or the other whether a U.F.O. had been sighted as there are still too many unknowns. Secondly, in the opinion of the writer such ventures are outside the main interests of this Division.

There are however two conclusions that are of interest to this Division, they are as follows:

(a) Radioactive contamination of rock and lichens was found at the alleged U.F.O. landing site. The origin of this contamination has yet to be determined.

(b) The radiation levels measured were not high enough to create a radiation hazard to the general public.

(Signed) S.E.H.

Report by Stewart Hunt on his visit to the site on July 27, 1967, with other RCAF members and RCMP, as well as Barry Thompson of CAPRO. While radiation levels of significance were found, the levels on this visit were not considered hazardous.

"A survey of the basement showed no evidence of any loose contamination. Radiation fields were detectable coming from the plastic bags containing soil and the remnants of Michalak's burned shirt... Mr. Michalak has no respect for contaminated materials. He handled the contaminated soil with his bare hands, and was made to wash his hands with great difficulty."
(Hunt 1967: 2)

Hunt was both horrified and suspicious. How could an amateur geologist and trained engineer not be concerned about radioactive debris? Hunt's visit was what helped convince Michalak to visit the site with Bissky and the others. Hunt went along to verify that radioactivity was present. He found that:

"One small area was found to be contaminated. This was located across the crown of the rock. There was a smear of contamination about 0.5 x 8.0 inches on one side of the crack. There was also some lichen and ground vegetation contaminated just beyond the smear. The whole contaminated area was no larger than 100 square inches. All water run off areas were checked for possible contamination, but nothing was found."
(Hunt 1967: 2)

After examining the site, Hunt felt there was "no serious health hazard involved," after all. The fact that only a small area was radioactive conflicted with the fact that Michalak's steel tape measure was radioactive, yet it was found "40 paces" from the site. The explanation offered for this was that everything taken from the site had been left together in a pile in Michalak's basement, so that unaffected items could have become contaminated after the fact.

In an undated Department of National Defence Minute Sheet, an official in the office of the Chief of Defence Staff in Ottawa noted:

```
                    INCIDENT REPORT

              CANADIAN FORCES OPERATIONS CENTRE

Time Reported   1310Z    Date    26 Jul 67   Person Reporting  Insp Headrick

Unit or Organization    RCMP Crime Lab

Location or Address    Ottawa                        Telephone  3 9367

Place of Occurrence

Time of Occurrence                          Z


Details    Re: Analysis of samples from Falcon Lake UFO Incident.
           Samples sent by RCMP to Dr A.H. Booth, National Health and Welfare, for
           radio-activity check.

           The report from Dr Booth indicates a radiation value of .3 microcuries
           in the soil sample.  Dr Booth reports that the radiation is from a
           radium source and is a possible serious health hazard.  He is sending
           an investigator to Falcon Lake area.

           Telephone number Dr Booth 7 4684


Injuries


Damage Report


Action Taken by Duty Officer

           Passed to Mr. E... Greenwood.
```

Report, noting the view of A. H. Booth, National Health and Welfare in Ottawa, on the analysis of the samples obtained by the RCAF and sent to the RCMP Crime Lab to check on radioactivity levels, dated July 26, 1967. The radiation at the site was considered a "possible health hazard" and was suggested to be produced by radium. This was likely one origin of the hypothesis that the site had been "seeded" with radium shaved from a luminous watch face or dial.

"There is some doubt that the soil samples did in fact contain '226' or pure radium. This question of doubt is a scientific evaluation beyond this investigation. The quantity of '226,' namely 0.5, is equal to approximately 1/3 of that associated with an average wrist watch. However, the quantity, although pertinent, does not explain how this 'smear' got on the rock at the alleged landing site. This is what is bothering the scientific people."
(Canadian Department of National Defence 1967)

Perhaps the most interesting aspect of the "radium seeding" scenario was Hunt's visit to the provincial Environmental Sanitation Laboratory in Winnipeg:

"Samples from [the] UFO site and those taken from Michalak's residence were checked under a UV light... The samples taken from the UFO site gave an indication that they were contaminated with Radium luminous paint. The samples from Michalak's house did not respond to the UV light."
(Hunt 1967: 3)

This was puzzling. If Michalak or Hart had seeded the radium, then they would surely have had some luminous paint in their own radioactive samples. Yet this was present only in the later samples.

Further confusing details were found when Hunt visited the home of Barry Thompson, the APRO investigator. Hunt checked some soil and vegetation samples Thompson had in his possession. Thompson had been given the samples by Michalak when he accompanied him during a separate visit to the site on July 17, 1967. Hunt noted that one sample:

"... proved to be radioactive. Levels up to 1mR/hr were detected... The sample was sealed in a plastic bag. A contamination check was made of the area where the samples were, using the UV light. The area was extremely cluttered with photographic equipment and a great deal of junk. Several areas responded to the UV light, but these did not prove to be areas of contamination, probably photographic emulsion splashes. Thompson appears to be a very sloppy worker."
(Hunt 1967: 5)

This raises the possibility that "emulsion splashes" were also the cause of the luminosity found in the RCAF samples from the landing site. Hunt learned that Thompson had given some samples to George Dyck, a technician at the Nuclear Medicine Department of the Winnipeg General Hospital. On his own time, Dyck had tested the samples using his department's standard laboratory equipment. One sample was said to have shown a "1.4 MeV peak" and two other weaker peaks. Hunt visited Dyck and was introduced to nuclear medicine specialist Dr. F. Helmuth, who had examined Michalak's burns when he had been brought in following his other medical tests. Hunt also interviewed other nuclear medicine specialists at the hospital. Dr. R. Walton, executive director of the Manitoba Cancer Clinic, was apparently embarrassed to have his organization involved in such tests because "they weren't particularly interested in becoming involved in work of this nature." The stigma of UFO investigation was too much for the medical establishment.

Between July 1967 and May 1968, the landing site was visited by a variety of individuals. One of these was Mr. E. J. Epp, who searched the area for radioactivity as part of a check by the provincial Department of Mines and Natural Resources. They were concerned that Michalak had misdirected the earlier searchers to protect his claims. However, not only did Epp not find any radioactivity, but Michalak didn't file any claims until the fall of 1967.

The lack of radioactivity at the time is important, because on May 19, 1968, Michalak again visited the site with a friend. In his report to the Condon Committee, Roy Craig said Michalak found:

> "... massive pieces of radioactive material in a fissure of the rock within the 'landing circle.' This ... consisted of two W-shaped bars of metal, each about 4.5 in. long, and several smaller pieces of irregular shape. These items were said to have been found about 2 in. below a layer of lichen in the rock fissure... the two fragments each consisted of a central massive metal portion which was not radioactive. One of these was 93% and the other 96% silver. Both contained copper and cadmium, and had a composition similar to that found in commercially available sterling silver or sheet silver. The metal was coated with a tightly-adhering layer of quartz sand, similar to that used as a foundry sand. This also was not radioactive. The radioactivity was contained in a loosely-adhering layer of fine-grained minerals containing uranium. This layer could be removed readily by washing and brushing. The minerals were uranophane and thorium-free pitchblende, characteristically found in vein deposits."
> (Condon 1969: 323)

In his own teletype to headquarters, Bissky said that when he examined the metal pieces at Michalak's home:

> "All shown objects were subjected to civilian Geiger counter and majority of readings at same level as that

of the dial face of a service wrist watch in same counter."
(Bissky 1968)

Again, there was speculation that radium was implicated in the radioactivity of the metal. It is ironic that it came from Bissky's own watch. Bissky also observed that:

"Larger objects appeared to have been cast for a specific design and Mr. M. indicated he had considerably more in his possession but would not allow viewing or indicate the exact numbers although he did allow that some were in a reverse 'S' design."

He then:

"... attempted knicking one of the larger pieces with a knife and found metal very resistant to knife although there was no normal metallic ring when struck by another metallic object or against a stone."
(Bissky 1968)

This last observation is curious, since a four-inch chunk of dense metal would not necessarily ring when struck. Bissky's concern that the matter still was very suspicious was obvious as he concluded:

"... should it be found metal is of unusual raw material, feel that NRC should be brought into picture for expert investigation. It may be that metals are normal large deposits of silver or other composite materials found in this area."

And, most importantly:

"… it is interesting that items have been located at exact point of alleged landing of UFO. Should this be a hoax, someone is going to considerable effort to perpetrate same."
(Bissky 1968)

An understatement, indeed!

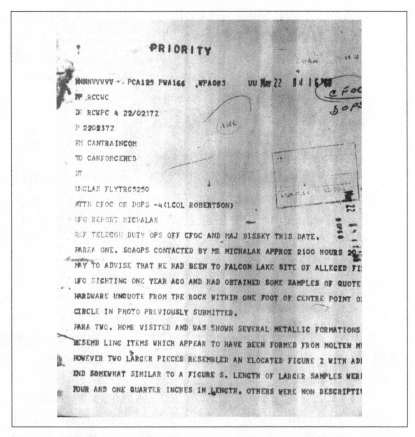

A year to the day of his experience, Michalak went back to the site with his colleagues and found the metal pieces deep in a crack in the rock floor. He dutifully reported his findings to the RCAF, and on May 22, 1968, this three-page telex was generated after investigators visited Michalak at his home to examine the metal. This is page one of the telex. Pages two and three are opposite.

THE FALCON LAKE CASE: A REVIEW

PAGE 2 RCMPC 4 UNCLAS

GLOBS OF METAL. COLOR IN THE MAIN WAS DULL SILVER WITH ORANGE OR BRONZE TINGE ON CERTAIN AREAS ON THE SIDES.

PARA THREE. ALL SHOWN OBJECTS WERE SUBJECTED TO CIVILIAN GIEGER COUNTER AND MAJORITY OF READINGS AT SAEME LEVEL AS THAT OF THE DIAL FACE OF A SERVICE WRIST WATCH ON SAME COUNTER.

PARA FOUR. LARGER OBJECTS APPEARED TO HAVE BEEN CAST FOR A SPECIFIC DESIGN AND MR M INDICATED HE HAD CONSIDERABLY MORE IN HIS POSSESSION BUT WOULD NOTALLOW VIEWING OR INDICATE THE EXACT NUMBERS ALTHOUGH HE DID ALLOW THAT SOME WERE IN A REVERSE S DESIGN BUT OF THE SAME GENERAL SIZE AS THE LARGEST ITEMS SEEN.

PARA FIVE. ATTEMPTED KNICKING ONE OF THE LARGER PIECES WITH A KNIFE AND FOUND METAL VERY RESISTANT TO KNIFE ALTHOUGH THERE WAS NO NORMAL METALLIC RING WHEN STRUCK BY ANOTHER METALIC OBJECT OR AGAINST A STONE.

PARA SIX. ATTEMPTED TO OBTAIN A SAMPLE FOR ANALYSIS BUT WAS REFUSED ALTHOUGH MR M INDICATED THAT HE MAY BE WILLING TO PROVIDE ONE SAMPLE ON A RETURNABLE BASIS ONCE HE HAD COMPLETED HIS OWN PERSONAL ANALYSIS , PERHAPS IN A FEW DAYS. HE DID VOLUNTEER THAT PHOTOGRAPHS OF OBJECTS COULD BE TAKEN IN HIS HOME FOR THE TIME BEING AND IT IS INTENDED TO MAKE ARRANGEMENTS TO HAVE THESE COMPLETED IN THE NEXT DAY AND WILL BE FORWARDED SOONEST

PARA SIX. NO INDICATIONS OF MAGNETIC FIELD IN ANY OF THE SAMPLES.

PAGE 3 RCMPC 4 UNCLAS

PARA SEVEN. MR M INDICATES THAT HE IS CONTINUING TO HAVE REOCCURRANCES OF HIS RED SPOTS ON HIS ABDOMIN AT APPROXIMATELY ONE HUNDRED AND TWENTY ONE DAY INTRVALS ALTHOUGH DECREASING INTENSITY.

PARA EIGHT. SUBJECT TO MR M ANALYISIS OF OBJECTS SHOULD IT BE FOUND METAL IS OF UNUSUAL RAW MATERIAL FEEL THAT NRC SHOULD BE BROUGHT INTO PICTURE FOR EXPERT INVESTIGATION. IT MAY BE THAT METALS ARE NORM LARGE DEPOSITS OF SILVER OR OTHER COMPOSITE RAW MATERIALS FOUND IN THIS AREA. HOWEVER IT IS MOST INTERESTING THAT ITEMS HAVE BEEN LOCATED AT EXACT POINT OF ALLEGED LANDING OF UFO. SHOULD THIS BE A HOAX SOMEONE IS GOING TO CONSIDERABLE EFFORT TO PERPETRATE SAME. AS LARGER METAL OBJECTS WERE LOCATED BY MR M AND AN ASSISTANT APPROXI 6 INCHES BELOW ROCK SURFACE IN A CREVISE WHICH HAD PREVIOUSLY INDICATED AN ABOVE NORMAL RADIO ACTIVE READING FOR SIZE.

PARA NINE ADVISE

BT

153

A number of institutions performed analyses on the metal pieces. Biospace Associates apparently had some samples tested through Colorado State University. They noted that:

"This particular alloy is made of silver, with no metallic impurities detectable by the x-ray fluorescence analysis." (Kachur 1968)

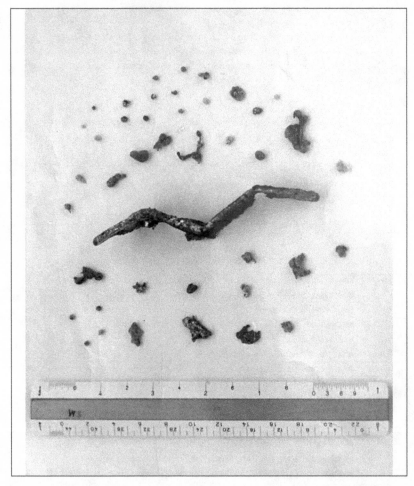

Some of the small silver pieces and one of the metal bars discovered by Michalak at the site in 1968.

In a note from the UFO Research Institute, located in Pittsburgh, Dr. J. Roesner reported that:

"The gamma spectra were complex; 15 distinct energies ranging from 0.11 MeV to 2.57 MeV could be resolved. The three major contributors to the total gamma radioactivity had energies of 0.61 MeV, 1.10 MeV and 1.53 MeV and decayed with half-lives of ~14 days, 8 days and 21 days, respectively... A semiquantitative chemical analysis... showed that 95 percent of the specimen is silver. The amount of copper in the specimen was determined to be 0.5 percent... The energies and half-lives of the gamma rays emitted by the specimen do not agree with the expected decay of silver activation products formed in an (n, g) reaction on natural silver."
(Weitzel 1968)

In his report to the Condon Committee, Craig quoted the conclusion of R. J. Traill, head of the mineralogy branch of the National Research Council of Canada, who reviewed the WNRE findings:

"I would interpret the specimen as pieces of thin sheet silver that have been twisted, crumpled, partly melted and dropped into or otherwise placed in contact with nearly pure quartz sand while still hot. They have subsequently been covered with loosely adhering radioactive material which consists of crushed pitchblende ore, much altered to uranophane and containing associated hematite."
(Traill 1968: 2)

Craig further noted:

"In view of the thoroughness of earlier searches of the site for radioactive material, it is improbable that the particles discovered a year later would have been missed had they been present when the earlier searches were made."
(Condon 1969: 323)

ATOMIC ENERGY OF CANADA LIMITED

CTB68-424

WHITESHELL NUCLEAR RESEARCH ESTABLISHMENT

MEMORANDUM

(A)

23 July 1968

TO : R. B. Stewart

FROM: J . D. Chen

Provincial Laboratory Samples

The following results were observed:

Sample	Activity Present
Native Silver	Uranium Ore Spectra
Unmarked Sample	"
Sink Product	"
Float Product	"
100 Mesh	"
60 Mesh	"
-60 + 100 Mesh	ND (activity too low)
-60 Mesh	"
Coarse Mineral Fragment	"
40 Mesh	Uranium Ore Spectra
Chared Fabric	"
Twig Fragment	"
Jack Pine Needle	ND (activity too low)

The gamma spectra showed an abnormally large 190 KeV photopeak which was thought to be due to enrichment of U^{235}. However chemical extraction for uranium of the 100 mesh sample and subsequent mass spectrometric analysis indicated that the samples containing uranium were of natural U^{235} content. Experiments are being continued to identify the cause of the large 190 KeV photopeak.

J. Chen

JDC/as   J. D. Chen

The silver was also analyzed at the national laboratory of the Whiteshell Nuclear Research Establishment at Pinawa, not far from Falcon Lake, operated by Atomic Energy of Canada. The AEC report was prepared on July 23, 1968.

However, CAPRO insisted otherwise:

"The fact is that there is overwhelming evidence that the metal was there, at least since July 1967. When the metal was located, and since it was taken from the middle of the rock, we examined the soil samples removed from the sight [sic] in July 1967. These samples also contained tiny fragments of the same metal and no doubt the samples taken by the authorities contain pieces as well."
(CAPRO 1969: 6)

Brian Cannon, a civilian investigator for CAPRO, was rightly concerned that the metal samples seemed to undermine the credibility of the case. It looked as if the metal bars were unrelated to Michalak's experience. To check this, CAPRO had the metal bars tested for the presence of radium. According to their report:

"Analyses confirmed the presence of Radium 226, the same source as was found in the soil specimens. The luminous watch dial paint theory dulled considerably."
(Cannon 1969c)

This latter point is particularly disturbing. Could experienced nuclear technicians have made such a mistake? The matter becomes more curious when one considers the results of reanalyses by Ufology Research of Manitoba (UFOROM) in 1977 and 1983. Soil samples allegedly from the Falcon Lake site were provided by a former CAPRO representative and tested for UFOROM at the University of Manitoba. The samples showed natural uranium activity but no radium signatures. This suggested that earlier indications of the presence of radium were in error.

In an internal Whiteshell Nuclear Research Establishment memorandum, lab analyst J.D. Chen reported on the analyses of "chared [sic] fabric," native silver, mineral fragments, twig fragments and jack pine needles. He wrote that:

> "The gamma spectra showed an abnormally large 190 KeV photopeak which was thought to be due to enrichment of U 235. However, chemical extraction for uranium of the 100 mesh sample and subsequent mass spectrometric analysis indicated the samples containing uranium were of natural U 235 content. Experiments are being continued to identify the cause of the large 190 KeV photopeak."
> (Chen 1968)

A further analysis of a soil sample was done in 1994 by UFOROM associate Greg Kennedy of Montreal. Gamma-ray spectroscopy found four radionuclides: U235, Pb214, Bi214 and Cs137. The cesium was probably due to fallout from nuclear weapons tests. Again, no enriched uranium was found, and no metal particles.

The soil was simply naturally high in uranium, a typical finding in the Whiteshell region. The original soil samples retrieved from the site contained only natural radioactivity. However, radium 226 was detected by some investigators. It is not clear whether or not this was an error. The metal samples, on the other hand, are definitely mysterious and do not appear natural because of their regular "W" bends.

INVESTIGATIONS

The most scientific report on the case was published by the infamous Condon Committee. Based at the University of Colorado which was awarded the contract by the United States Air Force, the Condon Committee was tasked with evaluating UFO cases for scientific value. Dr. Roy Craig and Mary Lou Armstrong of the University of Colorado both visited Michalak in June 1967. Accompanying them was John Fried of *Life Magazine*, which wanted to do a feature on the incident. Unfortunately, when Michalak tried to lead them to the site on June 4, he was unsuccessful.

As he explained:

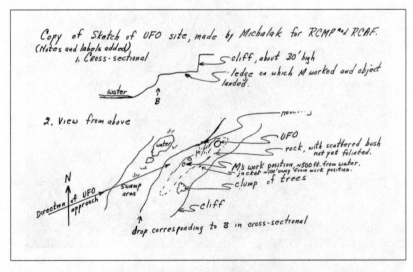

The sketch by Michalak of the site, made for the RCMP and RCAF, showing the vertical elevation of the site and its location in reference to the swamp, cliff and rock outcroppings.

"Nature changes quickly at that time of the year and the forest was very much different... than it had been when I was there before... The same thing happened later when the members of the RCAF... and the RCMP went with me to search for the spot. We even used a helicopter, but it was no use. It seemed as if the place had disappeared from the face of the earth."
(Michalak 1967: 29-30)

Stefan Michalak walking near the site in 1967.

Michalak noted that the investigators were "disenchanted" with his inability to find the site. Who could blame them? Their first visit was only two weeks after the incident, and already the story seemed to have a serious flaw. (It is probably because of this that the case was not regarded very highly by the Condon Committee and the USAF. Indeed, if *Life Magazine* had found the site, the story would have attracted much more attention and might have been more carefully documented.)

Access to Information requests by several people uncovered documents which provide more insight into the incident but also raise many more questions. In some cases, there are outright contradictions between civilian and government or military records of the investigations. The official RCAF report is undated but is thought to have been submitted in mid-June 1967 by Squadron Leader Paul Bissky.

Bissky noted he first led a search party to Falcon Lake on May 25, but could not find the site. On May 30, he visited Michalak to see if he felt well enough to accompany an investigation team. Michalak declined, but he drew a sketch of the area, described the site in detail and identified the likely area on an aerial photograph. On May 31, four RCMP, two RCAF and one other set of investigators in an H112 helicopter searched for the site, with no success. In his report, Bissky wrote:

"The RCMP returned to Winnipeg that evening and persuaded Mr. Michalak to accompany them to Falcon Lake the next day. Thinking he may be able to quickly locate the site from the air, Mr. Michalak was taken over the area by helicopter but he found no recognizable features. He stated he could probably do better on the ground. The search then proceeded with him leading the ground party, with the helicopter monitoring the proceedings from the air. With the aid of RCMP

portable radios, an air/ground link was possible and this greatly assisted in directing the ground party to the most likely-looking areas as described by Mr. Michalak. Following a frustrating afternoon and evening search... Mr. Michalak insisted the ground party had been very very close to the sought-after location as he recognized several physical features and areas where he had chipped rocks during his last prospecting visit."
(RCAF 1967a: 2)

It should be remembered that this was a joint investigation by military and police officers, armed with sophisticated rescue and detection equipment. Their search on June 2 was also unsuccessful. The RCAF team did not return to the area until July 28, when they had convinced Michalak to lead them to the site that he and Gerald Hart had found on June 25. In his supplemental report, dated September 1, 1967, Bissky wrote:

"Following an informal report from the RCMP to the effect that the samples submitted to CFHQ for analysis had proven to contain considerable radioactivity, and that a representative from the Dept. of National Health and Welfare was being sent out to investigate further, contact was made with all those concerned and a decision was made to a. Interegate [sic] Mr. Michalak again with the view to ascertaining the possibilities of his home and himself being contaminated by the materials which he brought out as samples; and b. Investigate the alleged landing site of the object, since Mr. Michalak had now been to the sight [sic] twice since his initial encounter. Although Mr. Michalak had previously been most uncooperative regarding taking either the

military or RCMP into the site, once the possible gravity and implications were made clear to him, he volunteered to lead a party into the area."
(RCAF 1967b: 2)

In other words, it was Bissky's opinion that Michalak did not want to take the officials to the site until they convinced him that radioactive contamination was a serious possibility. Michalak's distrust of officials and hesitancy was

Overhead view of Stefan Michalak at the site in 1967.

163

noted in Bissky's earlier report as well:

"When asked to provide the location of the site, Mr. Michalak objected very strongly on the basis that during his 25 June hunt he had in fact located what he had searched for originally and until such time as he could stake his claim, he had no intention of having anyone go near this area. It was pointed out to him that there was no intention of jumping his claim and that it was in the interest of the Canadian Public that he show the site to S/L Bissky. Mr. Michalak stated that no matter what anyone thought of him, he would not cooperate until his claim was filed. It turns out, however, that he now has to share his claim with his newfound partner, Mr. Hart, whom he had never met before. This was particularly surprising since he was very noticeably suspicious of the RCMP during the visit, so much so that he did not invite the RCMP into the basement to examine some [of] the latest samples brought back from the latest 'hot find.'"
(RCAF 1967a: Addendum)

However, when they finally did convince Michalak to lead them to the site on July 28, they were baffled by its appearance and location.

"Mr. Michalak successfully led the party to the sight [sic], in approximately 45 minutes going through considerable heavy bush, brush and undergrowth. The site was within 50 yards from where the ground party had searched on 1 June 67, but was not visible at that time because of the heavy bush located between the two areas."
(RCAF 1967b: 2)

In other words, there was a reasonable explanation

why the site had not been found by earlier searchers. This seemed to quell some doubts based solely on the inability to locate the site. They found:

> "... the outline of an approximate 15 foot diameter circle on the rock surface where the moss and earth covering has been cleared to the rock surface by a force such as made by air at very high velocity."
> (RCAF 1967b: 2)

The investigators took samples of the dirt, rock and vegetation and also examined trees within a few yards of the circle. This latter point was because there was some concern that the alleged size of the UFO (35 to 40 feet in diameter) would infringe upon several trees and saplings. There was no indication of burns or other 'disturbances.' This in itself was curious, since Michalak said he brushed against the craft, burning his glove. It seems logical that, at the very least, some leaves or limbs would have been seared or broken.

> "Considering the size of the alleged object (35-40 ft across), it is highly unlikely that it could have made a descent into and ascent from the area searched without having made contact with some of the surrounding trees. Even if it was not completely heated on the surface, there should have been some evidence of having brushed a tree or some bark removed. Yet there was no indication at all."
> (RCAF 1967b: 3)

One possible explanation is that the burned leaves fell and decayed during the two months since the event. None of the investigators were plant pathologists, so some evidence might have escaped them. However, some investiga-

Quartz vein running across the exposed rock floor of site. Michalak had been examining this feature and its position in relation to other features. This photo was taken in 2009 by Chris Rutkowski.

tors (and Michalak) insist that some trees were damaged and the evidence ignored. This is borne out by the following description of the site in the *CAPRO Bulletin*:

> "The clearing consists of three main outcroppings of rock covered with the usual covering of lichens and moss. One of these outcroppings, the one over which the object hovered, was pitted extensively and had slight radioactivity... The lichen and moss that covered the other rocks in the group was blown clear and was heaped in a ring around the edges of the rock over which the object was said to have hovered. A small tree which was growing through a crack in the rock had been bent and broken at the base and now lay on its side. The leaves of this tree discoloured in the following manner: on each leaf there was a round circle of brown within which was an area of red in the centre of which there was a hole. This sample was confiscated by the investigator sent by the National Research Council." (Cannon 1968: 4)

As this tree was not mentioned in the official report, this issue was never resolved. Although Craig had noted that there were no signs of any disturbances on the trees or other flora, when Michalak visited the site again in the fall of 1967, he found ample evidence that something had occurred there:

> "On September 30 I returned to the place where the craft had landed – to see if there were any other changes. I could not believe what I saw. The leaves in the area looked as if they had been sprayed with some killing chemical. All were withered and dead. No vegetation grew within a 50 foot radius of the landing site. The area where the craft had touched down was still visible."

(Michalak 1967: 36)

If someone had tried to make the site look "good," the embellishment of a circle of affected vegetation would certainly have been an excellent idea. What didn't escape the investigators was the complete absence of physical evidence besides the ring of debris:

> "... the complete removal of all evidence from the site makes it highly suspect that it was never there. One would have thought that some shreds or burned shreds or burned shirt particles would have remained, even after the two months elapsed time."
> (RCAF 1967b: 4)

Hart and Michalak appeared to have taken confirmatory evidence that might have bolstered the credibility of the story. However, had "burned shirt particles" been found, they would likely have been thought to be suspicious as well, perhaps planted by someone to support the case. One can ask whether or not any evidence would have been considered bona fide, given Bissky's personal conviction that the case was a hoax.

GOVERNMENT INTEREST

The Canadian government seemed to refuse access to information about the Falcon Lake incident when a question was raised in the House of Commons in 1967. On June 29, 1967, it was reported that a member of parliament, Edward Schreyer, asked about UFO investigations, specifically with regard to the Michalak case. The Speaker of the House immediately "cut off the subject without government reply." On November 6, 1967, Defence Minister Leo Cadieux stated:

"... it is not the intention of the Department of National Defence to make public the report of the alleged sighting."
(House of Commons 1967)

This was in response to requests by several cabinet members to obtain information on the incident. On November 11, 1967, Schreyer formally placed a written question on the Commons order paper seeking information on UFOs. However, the question did not solicit a useful response.

On October 14, 1968, House Leader Donald MacDonald again refused an MP, this time Barry Mather, access to reports on the Michalak case. However, on February 6, 1969, Mather was given permission by a member of the Privy Council to examine their file on UFOs "from which a few pages have simply been removed." It was claimed that outright release of the file "would not be in the public interest," and could create a dangerous precedent that would not "contribute to the good administration of the country's business."

(House of Commons 1969).

Science writer Yurko Bondarchuk (1979) reported that "portions of the complete government report are available for public scrutiny" at the National Research Council in Ottawa. However, "noticeably missing are the RCMP study of the burned items, as well as the government's final conclusion, if indeed one exists."

POSSIBLE CORROBORATIVE REPORTS

When Michalak's experience was covered by the local media, many people reported their own UFO sightings from around the same time and area. On May 19, 1967, just before his experience, residents of Lockport, near Winnipeg, reported a UFO with a "glowing ring of heat" moving at "indescribable speed." Just after his experience, on May 21, three people said they watched a "round reddish glowing object at treetop level" from their cottage not far from Falcon Lake at Eleanor Lake in the Whiteshell. They reported it to the RCMP on May 23, after Michalak's story was published. Later that month, two men watched a "large, cigar-shaped object travel across the horizon at a tremendous speed" on May 25. That same night, a large, orange, egg-shaped object was seen near Souris, and two other witnesses saw "two very brilliant stars in close proximity to each other" over Winnipeg. (All cases in UFOROM files.)

In 1978, a man contacted UFOROM with information about his encounter at West Hawk Lake one night in May 1967. Although he could not recall the exact date, he claimed it had occurred "the same time as Michalak." He and a companion were walking from West Hawk Lake to Caddy Lake along a highway. They had walked three of the four miles to their destination when his companion stopped to tie his shoelace. The man, looking straight ahead, was startled to see a large, disc-shaped object glide silently into view above the trees and move across the highway. It flew over the trees on the other side of the highway and was lost to sight. Needless to say, the man's companion did not look up

171

in time to see the object. The man's detailed sketch of the object had some resemblance to the Michalak's drawings, with some discrepancies.

In July 1992, a woman called UFOROM with information that she and her daughter had observed a UFO as they were travelling home from Falcon Lake along the Trans-Canada Highway the same weekend as the Michalak case. Around 4:00 p.m., they had left their cottage at Star Lake and were heading west when they saw a "perfect flying saucer" over the trees on the north side of the road. It was hat-shaped, with windows on its upper surface which were giving off "pinkish-mauve" light. The rest of the object was silver, and it appeared to be spinning counterclockwise. Her daughter sketched the object, and as they watched, it "disappeared into thin air." Independent sketches of the object by both witnesses agree in detail and seem to show a craft similar to that encountered by Michalak.

UNSOLVED MYSTERIES

In 1989, a producer of the NBC program *Unsolved Mysteries* contacted the Michalaks and other individuals for information relating to the Falcon Lake case. In June 1992, Mr. and Mrs. Michalak, their son Stan, and Chris Rutkowski, were flown by NBC to a remote set in South Dakota for a recreation of Michalak's UFO encounter. The segment aired on November 4, 1992.

On the air date, 22 calls were received by UFOROM and 20 were received by the NBC operators in California. None of the local calls provided any information directly relating to the Falcon Lake case, but seven callers reported their own UFO experiences. One caller reported seeing a bright orange light over Winnipeg "the same night as Michalak did." The next day, November 5, 1992, during a radio talk show in Winnipeg, one caller claimed that she was a former employee at the Whiteshell Nuclear Research Establishment at the time of the incident. She said that her supervisors candidly noted that the Falcon Lake site was "very radioactive." The *Unsolved Mysteries* segment was rerun on March 17, 1993, but no new solid leads were received.

CONCLUSIONS

In the report of the United States government-sponsored UFO project, Michalak's experience was described as "unknown," meaning there was no explanation. Their concluding remarks were impressive:

"... if [Michalak's UFO encounter] were physically real, it would show the existence of alien flying vehicles in our environment."
(Condon 1969: 323)

What really happened at Falcon Lake? There is no question that some level of radiation was found at the site where Michalak said he had his experience. As well, he did exhibit some very unusual ailments, including reported weight loss, peculiar burn marks on his chest and stomach, charred hair, an odd rash and recurrent dizziness.

Some UFO investigators have said he had met alien beings; some say he stumbled upon a secret government or military craft. Sceptics have proposed the only other explanation that would explain many of the facts: a hoax. The first published comment by sceptics about the incident was that by UFO debunkers Donald Menzel and Ernest Taves, who dismissed the case by noting:

"First, the project investigator and the prospector together were unable to locate the area of the happening. Second, the 'illness' appeared to have been caused by nothing more exotic than insect bites. And third, the

project's attempts to establish the reality event revealed 'many inconsistencies and incongruities' ... [Therefore] we regard the case as a badly executed hoax."
(Menzel and Taves 1977: 104)

Since the RCAF conceded that the site was difficult to find and since Michalak's illness was substantially more than insect bites, this dismissal appears somewhat abrupt. And, while there are certainly many incongruities in the case, these tend to heighten the mystery and not force dismissal by themselves. Even if the case was a hoax, it is not clear as to who might have been responsible, what was the motive, or the gain. In fact, even Bissky conceded the hoax was of a high calibre.

If it was a hoax, its execution was quite elaborate, as it fooled several different levels of investigation, and there are still many unanswered questions today. If the incident is a hoax, there are several possibilities for the identity of the perpetrator. If Stefan Michalak alone was the hoaxer, he would have needed many resources in addition to the stamina to stick to his story under intense questioning for more than 25 years.

The silver pieces found at the site are definitely suspicious. The hoaxer would have needed to visit the site at least once prior to the placement of the items in order to locate a suitable position to hide them. The hoaxer would also have had access to pitchblende ore and a way to cast the silver bars in order to give the appearance of 'found' objects. (For its re-creation of the incident, *Unsolved Mysteries* used an amalgam of solder and other materials to make convincing replicas of the metal pieces.) In addition, the hoaxer would have known that someone with a Geiger counter would return to the site so that the items could be discovered. Since the metal bars were not discovered after a thorough search of the area by

THE UNIVERSITY OF MANITOBA

DEPARTMENT OF GEOLOGY   WINNIPEG, CANADA

April 11, 1968

Dear Dr. Millman,

At our last meeting of the Meteorite Committee you mentioned the Falcon Lake Non Meteoritic Sighting. When I got home from Ottawa I found the local paper had an article on the latest or most up to-date account(??) of it and thought you might like to have a copy for your files. You can see that it must be an authentic "saucer" because of the drawing made at the site!!!!

Sincerely,

Edward Leith

While most investigators treated the case seriously, a few openly mocked Michalak and the evidence. Peter Millman, who was heading meteor studies at the National Research Council in Ottawa in the 1960s, was also in charge of its "Non-Meteoric Sightings File," where reports of UFOs ended up. He did not believe in aliens or UFOs as extraterrestrial spacecraft. Geologists and space scientists at post-secondary institutions across Canada assisted Millman's decidedly biased approach by sending him UFO reports from their regions. Edward Leith was head of geological sciences at the University of Manitoba at that time, and his correspondence with Millman on April 11, 1968, shows his contempt for the subject.

the official investigators in 1967, the hoaxer had several months to prepare the site for discovery by Michalak in 1968. During this period, dozens of persons could have had access to the site.

Other inconsistencies make the story problematic. It is interesting that the location of the encounter was within view of a forest ranger tower. Craig reports that the forest ranger on duty at the time of the incident reported he did not observe either the landing or flight of the UFOs, or the smoke which resulted from the ignition of vegetation. This would seem to flaw Michalak's story effectively, although the individual in the tower might not have been looking in the direction of the site constantly. But since the object was landed for at least 45 minutes, and if it gleamed in the sun or emitted an "intense purple light" (as it was said to have done), it is indeed puzzling as to why the individual in the tower did not see it.

Another problem that the Condon report noted was the direction in which the object departed. This direction was 255 degrees, which would have the object pass within a mile of the local golf course. No objects were reported by anyone from the golf course, although if the speed of the UFO had been great, this is not necessarily unusual. Craig noted that a northward-opening gap in the trees was inconsistent with the 255 degree bearing. However, Michalak clearly stated that the object rose vertically before departing.

If Michalak made the story up, why would he have gone to so much trouble to make it appear authentic? The Mayo Clinic psychiatric report concluded that Michalak was not the type of person to fabricate stories of this nature. If he had "fallen on a barbecue" (suggested by one sceptic) and burned himself while partying at Falcon Lake, why would it be necessary to claim it was the result of a UFO encounter? If he wanted to make it look good, would he not have made

177

sure the site was found easily, especially since *Life Magazine* was going to give the story publicity? A hoaxer of this calibre would certainly have wanted that kind of attention.

Another possibility is that Michalak had a real encounter with something, but someone else decided to improve the evidence so that the case seemed better. Given the number of people involved in both the military and civilian investigations, this is much more likely than a solo hoax attempt on Michalak's part. The problem is in the elimination of suspects.

Michalak's bill from the Mayo Clinic, dated September 3, 1968. He had a blood workup, x-rays, EEG and other tests, including the psychiatric examination, all for just over $400 USD. He paid it out of his own pocket, as the tests were not covered by Manitoba health insurance.

Finally, a note should be made about the use of hypnosis in the investigation of the case. CAPRO investigators located two clinicians who used hypnosis in their practices. In one of the earliest examples of hypnosis employed in ufology, Michalak underwent at least one hypnosis session in the late 1960s. A tape recording of a session was studied, but little information that Michalak had not already recalled consciously was uncovered during the session. (The issue is complicated by the fact that one of the alleged hypnotists denied that Michalak ever underwent hypnosis, yet the tape recording clearly indicates such a session took place.)

If we assume that Michalak's story is truthful, then we have a solid report of a landed UFO, complete with physical and physiological effects. Personal interviews with the Michalaks showed them to be sincere people. They were intelligent, levelheaded individuals, and well-read on many subjects. Their annoyance at their notoriety is apparent, and their defensiveness at repeated questioning showed that they had been subjected to severe ridicule and criticism after the incident first hit the media in 1967.

If officials were convinced Michalak was a hoaxer, why was he not prosecuted for public mischief? There was definitely evidence towards this end. It certainly would have been an interesting court case, arguing about the existence of UFOs.

It is even possible that Michalak would have won.

ACKNOWLEDGMENTS

It has proven very challenging to recover useful documents and piece together the Falcon Lake investigations. I would like to thank the following people for their kind cooperation and assistance in the preparation of this article: Roy Bauer, George Eberhart, Greg Kennedy, Maria Michalak, Stan Michalak, Stefan Michalak, Mark Rodeghier, Berthold Schwarz, Vladimir Simosko, and Michael Swords.

REFERENCES

Aggen, Erich A., Jr. (1969). Further Aspects of the Hostility Theory. *Flying Saucers*, No. 67 (December): 14-15.

Barry, Maurice J., Jr. (1969). Letter to Berthold E. Schwarz. April 1.

Bissky, Paul. (1968). Teletype to D. F. Robertson. May 22.

Bissky, Paul. (1980). Personal communication.

Bondarchuk, Yurko. (1967). *UFO Sightings, Landings and Abductions*. Toronto: Methuen. pp. 37-45.

Canadian Aerial Phenomena Research Organization (CAPRO). (1969). The Outcome of the Falcon Lake Landing. *CAPRO Bulletin*, Vol. 2 (January/February): 4-7.

Canadian Department of National Defence. (1967). "Confidential" Minute Sheet. Signed by D. F. Robertson. Undated.

Cannon, Brian C. (1968). UAO Lands at Falcon Lake. *CAPRO Bulletin*, Vol. 1 (January): 3-4.

Cannon, Brian C. (1969a). Strange Case of Falcon Lake, Part 1. *Canadian UFO Report*, Vol. 1 (March-April): 10-12.

Cannon, Brian C. (1969b). Strange Case of Falcon Lake, Part 2. *Canadian UFO Report*, Vol. 1 (May-June): 11-12.

Cannon, Brian C. (1969c). Strange Case of Falcon Lake, Part 3. *Canadian UFO Report*, Vol. 1 (July-August): 24-26.

Cannon, Brian C. (1970). Letter to Berthold E. Schwarz. January 24.

Chen, J. D. (1968). Memorandum to R. B. Stewart. July 23.

Condon, Edward U. (1969). *Scientific Study of Unidentified Flying Objects*. New York: Bantam. "Case 22," pp. 316-24.

Crain, T. Scott, Jr. (1971). Flying Saucer Casualties. *Flying*

Saucers, No.73 (June): 7-9.

House of Commons (Canada). (1967). *Debates*. November 6. Ottawa: The Queen's Printer. p. 3919.

House of Commons (Canada). (1969). *Debates*. February 6. Ottawa: The Queen's Printer. pp. 5234-36.

Hunt, Stewart E. (1967). *Determination of Possible Radiation Hazards to the General Public from the Alleged Landing Site of an Unidentified Flying Object near Falcon Lake, Manitoba*, in letter to A. K. DasGupta. September 13.

Kachur, Victor. (1968). Letter to Jim Lorenzen. September 26.

Lorenzen, Carol, and Jim Lorenzen. (1968). *UFOs Over the Americas*. New York: Signet.

McCampbell, James. (1987). Effects of UFOs Upon People. In: Hilary Evans and John Spencer (eds.), *UFOs 1947-1987: The 40-Year Search for an Explanation*. London: Fortean Tomes. pp. 200-210.

Mayo Clinic. (1968). *Psychiatric Report on Mr. Stephen Michallack* [sic]. August 6.

Menzel, Donald H., and Ernest H. Taves. (1977). *The UFO Enigma*. New York: Doubleday.

Michalak, Stephen. (1967). *My Encounter With The UFO*. Winnipeg: Osnova Publications.

Michalak, Stephen. (1980). Personal communication.

Naud, Yves (1978). *UFOs and Extraterrestrials in History*. Geneva: Editions Fermi. Vol. 3: 147-56.

Oatway, R. D. (1967). Confidential report for Dr. E. P. Cardera, CFB Winnipeg. September 19.

Oatway, R.D. (1968). Letter to Horace Dudley. March 22.

Rovelstad, Randolph. (1970). Letter to Berthold E. Schwarz. January 13.

Royal Canadian Air Force (RCAF) (1967). *Report of an Investigation into the Reported UFO Sighting by Mr. Stephen Michalak on 20 May 67 in the Falcon Lake Area*. Submitted by S/L

P. Bissky. Approx. mid-June.

Royal Canadian Air Force (RCAF) (1967). *Supplemental Report: UFO Investigation - Falcon Lake*. September 1.

Royal Canadian Mounted Police (RCMP) (1967). *Incident Report*. Canadian Forces Operations Centre. July 26.

Rutkowski, Chris. (1981). The Falcon Lake Incident: Part 1. *Flying Saucer Review*, Vol. 27, no. 1: 14-16.

Rutkowski, Chris. (1981). The Falcon Lake Incident: Part 2. *Flying Saucer Review*, Vol. 27, no. 2: 15-18.

Schuessler, John F. (1984). Cash-Landrum Case: Speculation about the Medical Effects. In: Walter H. Andrus and Dennis W. Stacy (eds.), *MUFON 1984 UFO Symposium Proceedings*. Seguin, Tex.: Mutual UFO Network. pp. 108-19.

Tokarz, Harry. (1978). Are UFOs Boon or Curse toMedicine? *Canadian UFO Report*, Vol. 4 (Summer): 8-11, 13.

Traill, R. J. (1968). Memorandum to S. C. Robinson. June 13.

Turner, W. (1967). Letter to Stewart E. Hunt. September 5.

Vezina, Allan K. (1968). Canada 1967 - A Big Year for UFO Research. *Flying Saucers*, No. 58 (June): 8-10.

Weitzel, William. (1968). Letter to Jim Lorenzen. October.

PART 5

Further Reflections on the Falcon Lake Incident

By Chris Rutkowski

In 1996, producers from the Arts & Entertainment TV network (A&E) contacted me to arrange a preliminary interview and work out details on their coverage of the Falcon Lake case for a series titled *Unexplained*. Only one show in the series was slated to be about UFOs, and there would only be five cases included. These represented, in their opinion, the cases with the best evidence and most accessible investigative background materials in the history of ufology.

Considering that this focus on the "best of the best" UFO cases was to include the Falcon Lake incident is very telling. Among the other cases on the show was to be the infamous Roswell UFO crash from 1947, often dramatized and portrayed in movies and TV shows such as the *X-Files*. If the Falcon Lake case was to be included among such noted events, it said something about the remarkable nature of Stefan Michalak's encounter with the UFO in the Manitoba's Whiteshell in 1967.

Originally, A&E said they were going to fly me down to their studios in June 1996, but that plan fell through because of scheduling problems and a change in producers. The new proposal was that the new A&E producer, Bill Neal, would fly into Winnipeg in mid-August to do some interviews and arrange some location shoots.

On Thursday afternoon, August 15, 1996, I met Bill at the home of Stan Michalak. Bill had been picked up by Steve Hladkyj, my friend who was at that time possibly the best videographer in the business. (Hladkyj had produced a TV special on the Manipogo monster that July, for which I was narrator and host.) Bill wanted to interview Stan Michalak because the elder Michalak was ill and not up to on screen appearances.

On camera for the A&E crew, Stan recounted how his family had been affected by his Dad's experience. Although he had been only nine years old at the time, he remembered the "neat" way TV and radio reporters had been appearing at seemingly all hours of the day and night, interfering with his life. He testified how sick his father had become and re-called seeing the burns on his Dad's body. He remembered especially "the smell like rotting eggs and burned electrical circuits which seemed to come out" of his father, "through his very pores."

Stan argued that there was no way his father could have made up the story and concocted such an elaborate hoax. "He was simply not that kind of guy," he said.

It's not generally known that Stan and I went to school together. I remember hanging out with him as a child and have a vague recollection that his Dad had been sick at one point, but when you're prepubescent, that kind of detail is not that important. We kept in touch through the years, occasionally crossing paths when he was an on air TV and radio personality. He's also a fine artist; his paint-ings of real life scenes are reminiscent of Edward Hopper and are clearly a result of his father's own talented genes. (Stefan Michalak's excellent landscape paintings are known only to a few insiders.)

In about 1975, when my interest in UFOs had reached a point where I began devoting much of my free time to in-vestigations and research on the subject, I had started col-lecting information about all known UFO sightings in Manitoba. I thought that that at least compiling a list of reports in one province could shed light on the nature of the UFO phenomenon across Canada. This became what is today the MANUFOCAT, which contains around 1,700 separate Manitoba UFO reports since about the year 1900.

While compiling the database, I realized that the Falcon Lake case was without a doubt the best and most well-documented in Manitoba, Canada, and perhaps in all the world. (It beats Roswell, in my opinion, since the U.S. government had always denied there was a UFO crash there, whereas Canadian authorities have documented the investigations at Falcon Lake and made them available in the National Archives.)

But what really happened at Falcon Lake? Was it possible that there was some detail missed by civilian UFO investigators that could still be uncovered, perhaps solving the mystery?

I reached out to my former classmate, to see if his family would be willing to have me talk with them about his father's experience. I knew that they were by then quite tired of media pestering them every time another UFO case was reported, seeking "the local angle."

I found that they had heard about some difficult events in my own personal life and had known my parents to some degree, as we were all part of the Winnipeg Polish community. They had even kept track of my work on the subject of UFOs and collected newspaper clippings in which I was mentioned in the context of investigations and scientific commentary. I was humbled as I found myself welcomed into their home, and their hospitality made me feel as if I was among my own family again.

I understood completely their view about media, as both Stan and I were involved in television and radio. Stan's parents were very "down to Earth" people who were not prone to flights of fancy. If anything, they were decidedly pragmatic.

The Michalak family was not eager to talk about the UFO experience again, but reluctantly conceded to talk with me since I was "practically family." I spent many hours discussing various aspects of Mr. Michalak's UFO encounter in their living room, while his wife served coffee to us and more often than not interjected with commentary of her own.

But that was many years in the past, and when A&E wanted to interview Mr. Michalak, he was no longer up for it. So when they appeared in Winnipeg in 1996, it was on Stan Michalak's patio where they began their series of recorded interviews.

Steve Hladkyj set up the camera on Stan's patio with his friend Greg as the sound man. Bill interviewed Stan for about an hour, carefully getting him to cover several important points. I hung around as the gopher.

I had urged the original A&E producer to also interview Peter Warren, an investigative journalist with an abrasive on-air radio personality but with a warm, witty personae underneath. Peter had been the news editor at the *Winnipeg Tribune* when Stefan Michalak contacted him to relate his story, and I thought Peter would be an excellent "character witness" since he had always supported Michalak whenever he was mentioned in media over the years.

However, somewhere in the planning process, Peter was dropped from the list of interviews. I told Bill that Peter would still be a good person to get on camera, and he asked me to see if Peter was available. As it happened, Peter had been out that day, investigating a story for his show, and didn't return until suppertime. But since the interview with Stan took longer than expected and Steve also had to shoot some still photos and maps, by the time that was done Peter was available.

We zipped out to Peter's house: a beautiful, well-appointed home with a large well-manicured front yard and a lush green backyard that dropped steeply down to the river. Inside, a baby grand piano sat in an atrium next to the patio and deck, adjacent to the bright, open and well-stocked kitchen. While we waited for Steve and Bill to arrive, Peter offered me a glass of his homemade wine and we chatted in his living room.

The conversation was so absorbing, before I realized it, we had finished the bottle. It took a while for the others to arrive, as Steve had lost me in traffic. When they finally appeared in the driveway, we quickly assisted them with unloading their gear and helped them set up on the deck overlooking the river.

Steve got the camera set up and when the light and sound was checked, Bill asked Peter what he remembered about the case. Bill commented to me later that in his opinion, Peter was "fantastic." His glowing comments about Michalak's character were almost too flattering. At one point, Bill asked him if he thought Michalak might have been lying about his experience, and Peter pointed his finger angrily at Bill. "You'd be more likely to be scamming me than Steve Michalak!" he retorted.

It was obvious that Bill was very impressed with the Michalak case. He could not understand why it had not received more attention from researchers and did not consider the possibility that Michalak had hoaxed the incident. However, he did say he expected sceptic Roy Craig, who in 1967 had investigated the case on behalf of the United States Air Force's Condon Committee, to "probably come up with something" when he interviewed him in the coming weeks.

The next morning, the A&E crew picked me up at my home just outside of Winnipeg. From there, it was an easy hop onto the freeway straight out to Falcon Lake. Steve drove the van, with his brother-in-law Terry beside him. (Terry was hired to be the actor playing the role of Stefan Michalak in the re-creation of the event on film.) Greg and Bill were in the row behind them and I was assigned to the back of the van.

During the two-hour trip into the Canadian Shield, we talked about where we would go and how we would approach the shoot. Bill wanted to find a nice open area in which to film the re-creation of Michalak getting burned. The plan was to actually set a mannequin wearing a shirt on fire, and make up Terry to look as if he had been injured. I didn't think that setting a fire inside a park was a good idea, especially during a forest fire season. Bill then suggested doing it in a campground, but eventually decided it would be best to do it on private property where government and park regulations would not apply.

We arrived at Falcon Lake right at noon and proceeded directly to the parking lot of the Falcon Creek hiking trail. I recommended that we park there and hike into the area near the main creek, less than a kilometre up the trail. Since the A&E expedition was not designed to actually reach the exact site but only to find a suitable area for filming a re-creation, locating and setting up at the actual site was not necessary.

Our group traveled up the trail about a quarter of a mile, over a bridge, across rocks, past a boulder the size of a mobile home, through dense underbrush and finally out onto immense, flat shales (slates?) lit by the bright sun. After a brief survey of the area, Bill decreed that one flat area was perfect for the shoot and that the natural lighting was optimal, so we stopped and set up the gear.

The first step was to recreate Michalak examining some rocks for signs of silver or other ores, as he was doing while prospecting back in 1967. Stefan Michalak had staked some claims in the area, searching for evidence of silver or gold. In fact, gold was discovered in the Whiteshell in 1911, and the Bissett gold mine is only about 150 kilometres away. Although it closed in 1983, it reopened in 2016, so there has been some renewed hope for amateur prospectors looking to strike it rich.

As we stood looking around the area in 1996, we saw a natural cleft in a rock at the side of one flat spot, so that's where Steve set up the camera. Terry donned a cotton under-shirt and plaid shirt that matched Michalak's old clothing, then added the old-style cap, goggles and rubberized gloves. A little talcum powder added to his hair by Steve and me, and Terry looked somewhat like a fifty-year-old Michalak.

The shooting went very well, although scenes were done over and over again, and from several angles, with close attention paid to continuity. The one scene where Michalak first sees the UFO must have taken two hours by itself. Then, it was time to film the fun stuff: Michalak touches the side of the craft and is burned by exhaust as it lifts skyward.

We weren't going to do the pyrotechnics there, so Terry simply re-enacted getting knocked down by the exhaust and getting burned. For the close-ups of his body, I used oil pas-tels to skillfully create singes, charring and burns on Terry's chest and stomach to match those that appeared on Micha-lak's body.

Terry effectively faked being blasted with hot gas: rolling, staggering and acting disoriented while Steve did hand-held close-ups and POV (point-of-view) shots, follow-ing him as he moved around. Greg ran along beside them with the boom mike, capturing every one of Terry's moans and gasps.

After what seemed an eternity, it was finally time for my part. I wasn't part of the re-creation, but Bill wanted to interview me out at Falcon Lake for authenticity and at least an air of credibility. We found a relatively flat patch of rock and Greg miked me up. Bill sat across from me and when Steve had the camera in place, began asking me about my involvement with the case and my view on what had really happened.

As I explained on camera that day, the major sticking points for the few outspoken skeptics of the case are: the inability for Michalak to find the site in the company of *Life Magazine* and the Condon investigators; some apparent discrepancies in Michalak's story; and the view that Michalak's physiological effects were nothing more serious than insect bites.

The third objection is the easiest to deal with; Michalak's injuries were much more serious than insect bites, and the rashes which later appeared could not conclusively be explained as allergic reactions. Michalak had second-degree burns on his upper chest, plus the "checkerboard array" of red spots that corresponded to the "exhaust grid" he had seen on the side of the craft. Although the spots faded after a while, even decades later, he had invited me to touch his abdomen, where I could easily feel the scar tissue underneath his skin. He must have been standing very close to the exhaust for the directed blast to create such a precise pattern on his body. Most exhaust vents I have seen have a great deal more spread upon release, so these were apparently some kind of needlepoint jets of hot gas.

The rashes were more than simple insect bites, too. Michalak had lesions on his legs as well as his upper body, and examining doctors documented them in detail. These seemed to have been caused by Michalak falling backwards from the blast of gas, with bent knees. Since we have the medical records of Michalak's own doctor, plus the Mayo Clinic records, it is easy to see that there were significant medical complications following his UFO encounter.

The second objection isn't that much of a problem, either. Michalak's basic testimony didn't change significantly between his first interview and the time of his death in 1999.

The only real incongruities were those which arose during the various civilian, military and other official investigations, such as the hotel bartender's testimony that was at odds with other evidence. In fact, a point I have made repeatedly is that while Michalak referred to the UFO encountered as a "space craft," he did not mean he believed it was piloted by aliens. He was of the opinion that it was some kind of American (or Soviet) secret landing vehicle, perhaps in testing for a Moon landing. Michalak certainly did not believe in "little green men,"

There remains the issue of finding the site, however. The site is not all that easy to locate, even with good orienteering skills. The trees all look the same, and in 1967, there were no trails in or out. Rock faces would have appeared similar and the terrain is fairly rugged. Furthermore, Michalak was still very ill when he was asked to lead the official expedition. It can be argued that these and other factors could have made finding the site more of an effort than had been thought.

But to the contrary, the main expedition included members of the RCMP as well as RCAF, and one would think that they would be pretty good at wilderness orienteering. Finding a thirty-foot circular patch of radioactive vegetation should have been a piece of cake. Of course, according to the map in RCMP files, the team was to search an area of twenty square miles.

Curious, also, is Craig's claim that Michalak suggested the search be called off only an hour or so after they started, shortly after noon. Given that they still had another four or five hours of daylight at that time of year, that is a bit odd. But given that Michalak was ill and was tiring easily, it could be explained. As I noted earlier, Michalak must have been very disoriented after his encounter to wander so far west of the site before reaching the highway.

The first time I was taken to the site was in the company of CAPRO members who led me with a large party into the bush around a great swamp before we reached what I was told was the location. We took measurements and samples and went back to Winnipeg, but the next day I was told we had actually been at the wrong spot because the guides had lost their bearings. I went back with a friend later that year and did find the location after some orienteering and some luck. After that, I could find the site with some confidence by walking along an established trail and veering away from the well-worn path when it went across a rock outcropping and through a large patch of blueberry bushes in season. Since then, the Falcon Beach Riding Stables has been taking tourists on a "UFO Ride" directly to the site on horseback as a local attraction.

The fact that the site was found by Michalak and a family friend a few weeks after the government officials had failed to do so later can indeed suggest to sceptics that the site only existed after he had "created" it himself as part of a hoax. But would the RCMP and RCAF not have checked Michalak's movements previous to his finding the site and tried to pin a public mischief charge on him if they were convinced he was having them on? The numerous searches must have cost a great deal of money at the time. Michalak could have been prosecuted for a false claim, if officials were convinced he had fabricated the whole event.

Furthermore, what could a hoaxer have been doing in the wilderness that could have resulted in a peculiar pattern of chemical and heat burns? Why go to the media with a story that couldn't have been supported? Why not just shut up about the whole thing? So many aspects of the hoax theory don't add up. It raises more questions than it answers.

Anyway, during the filming, I answered Bill's questions as best I could, saying that I did not think the case has been satisfactorily explained. Maybe a clever editor could have had me say that it was a prelude to an *Independence Day* sequel, but there's always a danger of that when dealing with media.

After my interview, we packed up and headed out of the woods. Bill had an idea that the riding stable's owner might allow us to film on his property. He went into the office while I went over to the stable, where a teenage girl was getting some horses ready for riding. She asked me what we were doing and I told her we were doing a piece about the guy who was burned by a UFO.

"Oh, you mean the place on the ridge," she said. "I've been there lots of times."

Apparently, the place is a Mecca. Everyone in the area knows about it. In fact, a UFO buff once organized a public trip out to the site that attracted nearly 150 tourists and hikers. Unfortunately, according to some people at the riding stable, "the crowd really made a mess of the site" that day.

Bill returned with the owner of the riding stable, who agreed to let us film in the parking lot. The first order of business was to shoot a close-up of gas jetting out of the UFO's exhaust grid. Bill and Steve had cleverly manufactured this with a cookie sheet and a fire extinguisher. Steve had found a rusted cookie sheet, polished it clean and drilled an array of one-inch holes in its surface. It was mounted on a tripod and Bill held a CO_2 fire extinguisher behind it. The recreation of the blast took several tries.

Then it was time for the action shots of Terry (as Michalak) being blasted, with pieces of a smouldering shirt and torched vegetation as added effects. I now fully understood the reason for the fire extinguisher.

Bill spotted a rock face and scrambled up a cliff to the top of a ridge about twenty feet up, just beside some log cabin-style cottages. He declared it a good spot and we went to get the gear. Terry and I had stuffed another shirt with yellow insulation. The idea was to use a blowtorch to start it on fire then bat it out with gloved hands and leave it smouldering. We did this all on the ridge, with amused cottagers looking down on us (literally and figuratively).

The first series of shots, though, included having Terry on the ground and getting blasted with the fire extinguisher "smoke." Steve used handheld shots to make the effect more dramatic. I had to admit that it looked pretty good, for Roger Corman, the noted low-budget sci-fi movie director. (True fact: the A&E producer's son had actually worked for Corman.)

Then Steve and I set up the stuffed shirt and Terry lit the torch. The shirt burned easily... too easily, which was when we found out that Bill shouldn't have done so many takes of the exhaust grid shot. All we got was a gasp of air when the fire extinguisher lever was pressed, because it had run out of charge. We ended up stomping on the shirt and the moss which had also ignited. On the tape, though, this all looked rather impressive. With proper editing, Bill thought the entire re-creation would look fine.

Finally, the shoot was over for the day. It was nearly 7:00 pm and we had missed both lunch and dinner. Steve had to return the camera equipment by about 8:30 pm, so we packed up and headed back to Winnipeg.

On the way back, we discussed the case, and Bill agreed that the site would not have been that easy to find. If Michalak was a hoaxer, P.T. Barnum should thank him for his groundbreaking efforts. If he had a real experience, the case was very puzzling. Perhaps the initial sighting was *bona fide* but a UFO buff fabricated a lot of the evidence in order to make it seem more robust. If one was into conspiracies, it could even be suggested that the military had created the site and muddied the effects to cover up a real landing of something. (After all, their investigation was hardly thorough or objective.)

In retrospect, being directly involved with an outside view of the Falcon Lake case gave me a new perspective on the incident. Although I have done a lot of research on the case, I appreciate now how much more can be done and also what is missing from the original investigation reports. For example, where exactly did Michalak emerge from the bush? What exact path did Michalak take out of the woods? Steve Hladkyj noted that a real police investigation would have tried to track Michalak's movements between the time of his encounter and the time he found the site, in order to rule out his tampering.

As skeptical as I am of most UFO cases, the Falcon Lake case is intriguing. All things considered, it's a very strange case. If it is a hoax, it's got enough complications to make it one of the best on record. In fact, I argue that the Falcon Lake case is better that the infamous Roswell Crash, since government officials accept that something actually happened at Falcon Lake, unlike Roswell. The site is locatable. There were physiological as well as physical effects, and we have literally hundreds of official documents detailing the investigation of this fascinating incident, unlike Roswell.

From a scientific perspective, I can only judge a case on the available evidence. There is, of course, no explicit proof that the object Michalak encountered was a flying saucer. It could have been a military test craft of some sort, which might explain the official interest in the case and why their detailed investigation seems incomplete to civilians.

All we have is a record of actual injuries to a man who claimed he was burned by a close encounter with a strange craft in a sparsely-populated part of the Canadian Shield. It's a single-witness case, yet it does come with some physical evidence. It may be inconclusive evidence, but it's there nevertheless.

Michalak's family supported him completely. Wouldn't they have grown tired of the whole charade after all these years and called him on it? They gained nothing and suffered greatly. With all the attention and the number of people involved in the case over the years, wouldn't an accomplice have finked on them at one point?

What really happened at Falcon Lake on May 20, 1967?

REFERENCES

Bondarchuk, Y. (1979). *UFO Sightings, Landings and Abductions*. Methuen, Toronto. pp. 37-45.
Campagna, P. (1997). *The UFO Files*. Toronto: Stoddart.
Michalak, S. (1967). *My Encounter With The UFO*. Winnipeg: Osnova Publications.

PART 6

Epilogue or Interlude?

By Chris Rutkowski
with Stan Michalak

More than 50 years have passed since Stefan Michalak reported his experience at Falcon Lake. Both the RCMP and Canadian Forces closed their case files on this a long time ago, labelling it "Unexplained."

That's not to say that nothing has been happening since investigations wound down and interest in the incident waned. The case is still considered by ufologists as one of the best on record, although most UFO buffs today haven't even heard of it.

A few months' previous to the release of *When They Appeared*, I contacted journalist Kevin Rollason of the *Winnipeg Free Press* to see if there was any interest in covering the 50th anniversary of an event that had become part of local history and lore. He didn't need much convincing. In fact, he thought the story deserved a feature treatment.

A week before the 50th anniversary, Rollason and a photographer travelled with me and Stan Michalak to Falcon Lake. I had been there several times, but Stan had never actually been to the site of his father's experience.

We went directly to Falcon Beach Ranch, where its owner Devin Imrie had several horses saddled up and ready to head north-east into the forest. After a 45-minute ride around swamps and across rocky ridges, our guide led us to the site where Stefan Michalak said he encountered the UFO.

Stan was overcome with emotion. He brought a copy of his father's sketch of the area from 50 years ago. The sketch matched the lay of the land, from the ridge to the large flat rock, and from the swamp to the sloping "landing site." Even the directions to the openings in the trees and the sight line to the north made perfect sense, based on the site map that Michalak drew just days after the encounter and had given to the RCMP before they attempted to find the site on their own. Stan was convinced, and emotional.

> "He was here. It was a phrase I repeated as I moved from place to place on the rocky outcrop. The map I held exactly described the terrain I was seeing. The compass notation even matched when I checked it against a compass I had brought. Oddly enough, Devin mentioned that the beavers had dammed up a lot of creeks nearby which flooded the swamp to the northwest of us resulting in a body of water that would have looked very similar to the pond from which the geese had made such a racket in 1967.
>
> "I felt my dad was vindicated. Even if I discount the craft as extra-terrestrial, the fact that I had proof of his presence on this remote piece of the Canadian Shield told me that the encounter happened, even though we will always question what it was he encountered.
>
> "I can admit that the tears came freely. Because of dozens of excuses, some of them legitimate, I had never come to this place. Now that I was here, I was overwhelmed."

Rollason wrote a long piece on the trip that became a front page story about the anniversary, with three full pages of coverage inside, plus photos from the site. Response to the story was tremendous, with many comments of support.

The news coverage led to an overfull crowd on hand at the launch of *When They Appeared* at McNally Robinson Booksellers in Winnipeg. Interest was so high that all available copies of the book were bought before Stan and I even began speaking and taking questions from the huge audience. Those who lined up after the event had to settle for signed bookplates that could be inserted into copies of the books when a new print run had been completed during the next week. In fact, the book remained on the McNally Robinson Best Seller List for eight weeks – rare for a local book.

One of those in the crowd for the book launch was a man who greeted Stan with a rare copy of Stefan Michalak's original booklet *My Encounter With the UFO* from 1968. The visitor had opened the booklet to show a photo of the RCMP team that had accompanied Stefan Michalak to the site in 1967. Pointing to one of the men in the photo, he said, "That's me!"

Chris Rutkowski (left) and Stan Michalak (right) visit the remote site of the Falcon Lake UFO incident in May, 2017.

Unfortunately, because of the large number of people surrounding us, Stan could only talk with him for a few moments, and the man left before we could get his contact information.

However, in 2018, I was able to find him. Cpl. John ("Jack") Zacharias was the partner of Cpl. Gerry Davis in 1967, investigating the Falcon Lake case for the RCMP. Zacharias had retired as an RCMP inspector after a long and remarkable career that had taken him literally around the world. He had moved to British Columbia following his retirement and had only moved back to Manitoba relatively recently. His presence at the book launch surprised Stan.

> *"I was stunned. My wife took a photo of me in the moment, and we still laugh when we see the shocked expression on my face. Here was a living witness to the events of 1967 at a time when I thought we would be lucky to find anyone who had a hand in that investigation. There he stood – a handsome man with a rugged but friendly face topped with a wave of white hair and, if that wasn't enough, he showed us candid photos taken at the time while Dad and the RCMP were at the site.*
> *"I had never known him as Jack; he was always Constable Zacharias to a polite nine-year old. He even corrected me on Corporal Davis' first name which is shown on one official document as Jim and in another as the initial J. It is how we introduced him in our book, but Jack said it was Gerry. Perhaps the J referred to the other spelling – Jerry. The little details like that make this story personal, and I was glad to have made such a personal connection."*

Zacharias recalled his investigation of Stefan Michalak's story very vividly. He remembered visiting bedridden Michalak soon after his experience, and he recalled thinking that he did not have an explanation for the incident.

Zacharias noted that the investigation of the case was particularly memorable for another reason that was unrelated to the UFO. The RCMP investigating team had flown to Falcon Lake from Winnipeg in a transport helicopter, and on their return trip, they had engine trouble. The pilot was forced to make a fast emergency landing, and the only flat area near them was on the Trans Canada Highway.

"It made me nervous," he said. "And then after we made the emergency landing, they had to call for a transport from Winnipeg to come pick us up."

Corley Sweeting is the owner of The Laughing Loon in the town of Falcon Lake, and chairman of the local Chamber of Commerce. He is a big supporter of the case, and has organized public presentations about it. His store carries many souvenirs of Falcon Lake, especially items describing the UFO encounter, including t-shirts, hats, keychains, bumper stickers, and mugs. One issue that he says needs addressing is the lack of signage in the area commemorating the 1967 event.

"You can drive right by along the Trans Canada Highway and not know that the UFO was seen here," he explained.

It's true that although the site is reachable, there isn't a sign along the highway noting Michalak's infamous encounter there, nor is there a commemorative cairn, plaque, or marker indicating a site of historic significance.

For the past few years, the town of Falcon Lake has organized a "UFO Encounter Weekend" in May to recognize the incident, attracting hundreds of visitors. A question often asked by tourists is the location of a plaque or sign on the highway, or near the actual site, similar to that of other historic places in Canada.

It is easy to see that the Falcon Lake UFO Encounter is part of Manitoba's cultural history, and perhaps nationally as well. With this in mind, discussions have been taking place regarding the recognition of the incident with some kind of permanent historic marker.

Such recognition for a UFO case is not without precedent. Most people have heard of the alleged "Roswell UFO Crash" in New Mexico in 1947. The Roswell Chamber of Commerce has embraced the story fully and the town celebrates the case each year, with many markers and signage. In Canada, the equivalent to Roswell is the story of a UFO crash near Shag Harbour, Nova Scotia, in 1967. Businesses and townspeople there were able to secure funding for a permanent sign on the highway near the site, developed a museum, erected a plaque, and hold an annual UFO celebration that attracts tourists from around the world.

Today, more than 51 years after the Falcon Lake UFO encounter, the need for a permanent and public roadside attraction commemorating the event is obvious. The story fascinates fans of the subject, and whether one is a believer or a skeptic, it still attracts attention and discussion. Public interest about the incident remains high, and the area would benefit from more tourist traffic.

For these and other reasons, conversations with government and commercial institutions are underway to create some kind of acknowledgement of the Falcon Lake UFO encounter as a Canadian historical event.

In a way, this has already occurred. In the spring of 2018, the Royal Canadian Mint issued a commemorative $20 coin depicting the incident, effectively denoting it as of national significance. The Mint had contacted Stan in 2017, detailing plans and design of the coin. He and I discussed the design and eventually approved a revision that became the imagery cast in silver.

"When I was contacted by the Royal Canadian Mint, I was at a loss for words, and I'm sure I stumbled and stammered during the conversation about what was being proposed and how it might turn out. Chris and I had thought about a lot of things, but this was certainly not on our radar. The initial design was good, but the UFO depicted in the artwork looked nothing like the craft my father had drawn. So, we made some tweaks and the result turned out better than I expected. I think Dad would have been happy to see his encounter commemorated in this way, and I have no doubt he would have found the irony in seeing the event on a coin made out of silver."

As a novelty item as well as a commemoration, the coin is physically shaped in the form of an ovoid alien face. Its reverse side shows a coloured rendition of the Falcon Lake UFO hovering over Stefan Michalak; when a black light projector (supplied with the sale of the coin) shines on the image, a beam of glowing green light appears to play upon

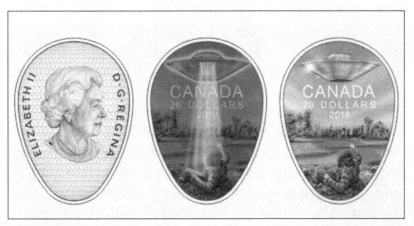

A black and white image of the coloured coin depicting the Falcon Lake UFO incident released in 2018, showing the obverse side, then the effect of the black light on the reverse side, and the unlit coin.

Image courtesy of the Royal Canadian Mint

the figure of Michalak. The Queen is on the obverse side, of course. The release of the coin attracted so much international attention, the entire run of 4,000 was sold out within 24 hours.

The story of Stefan Michalak's UFO encounter continues to evolve and impact Manitobans in amazing ways. In April 2018, Stan and I were invited to the world premiere of a newly commissioned choral work based on the story.

Burns from Beyond was premiered on April 29, 2018 before a full house at a concert in Ile des Chênes, Manitoba, performed by musicians and the Seine Singers choir, directed by Arlene Schulz. Its composer, Stephen Haiko-Pena, noted he had "always been aware of the 1967 sighting, having spent childhood summers at Falcon Lake" at his family's cottage. He had read *When They Appeared* and said he had been "devouring it at the time Arlene Schulz asked me to write something for her choir." He found the three main parts of the book (Stefan's story, Stan's story, my analysis) were effective in bringing the event to life from three completely different angles.

Haiko-Pena explained: "I based the first four movements of my work on Stefan's account, while the fifth movement is titled 'Corroborating Reports' and refers to reports from Chris' chapter and other sources."

Burns from Beyond is scored for women's choir and band (piano, flute, fiddle, guitar, bass, drums). The first movement is "Victoria Day Long Weekend, 1967," an instrumental in doo-wop style to suggest the leisurely beach culture and provide a calm before the storm. The second movement is titled simply "Stefan Michalak" and is a polka, referring to Stefan's heritage and telling the story of Stefan's life up until the moment of the encounter. Next is "Two Cigar-Shaped Objects," the focal point of the piece, featuring startled geese, voices from within the craft, and the injuring of Stefan all presented musically. A soloist speaks to the craft in five different languages. The fourth movement is "The Sickness That Followed," with a relentless beat depicting Stefan's bewildered journey through the bush and back to civilization. Finally, "Corroborating Reports" is a lilting minuet with three soloists who describe other Manitoba UFO sightings before the chorale reaches its climax with the chorus: "Steve, we believe!"

"My family had always been surrounded by music. To witness a musical acknowledgement of Dad's story was moving, humbling, and I'm sure my mother heard every note."

And that's where the story of Stefan Michalak's experience rests...at the moment. For those who find the entire notion of UFOs unpalatable, the case offers nothing in the way of incontrovertible evidence of alien visitation. For those fascinated with the lore and mythology that has risen from the many UFO reports over the past several decades, the Falcon Lake case is rich in detail, ranging from personal observation to cultural effects.

"I wanted to put this story in its proper perspective: told from the family view and from the unbiased view of sound reporting and record collecting for which I can never thank Chris enough. My father's encounter changed our lives and, now that the tale is told without the inaccuracies of the Internet, supposition or exaggeration, I believe I can be content knowing that I have made peace with the past and with the memories of my father, mother and brother."

For me, it's story that still invokes a sense of wonder.

APPENDIX A

The report filed by
Constable G.A. Solotki of the
RCMP Falcon Beach Detachment
to RCMP D Division
on June 16, 1967

ROYAL CANADIAN MOUNTED POLICE REPORT
D Division
16 June 67
Falcon Beach Highway Patrol
Stefan MICHALAK
Report of Unidentified Flying Object
Falcon Beach, Manitoba - 20 MAY 67

1.   At approximately 3:00 PM, this date, I was patrolling PTH#1, one half mile West of Falcon Beach, Manitoba, when I noticed a man walking on the South shoulder of the highway, towards Falcon Beach. He was wearing a grey cap, brown jacket with no shirt, light coloured trousers and carrying a brown brief case.

2.   This subject, upon seeing the police car, began waving his arms excitedly. I turned around on the highway and drove back to see what he wanted. He shouted to me to stay away from him. I asked him why and he replied saying that he had seen two space ships. He said I might get some sort of skin disease or radiation if I came too close. He seemed very upset. I asked for some identification and he gave me a document pertaining to prospecting, which showed his name as Stefan MICHALAK of 314 Lindsay Street, Winnipeg, Manitoba.

3.   I enquired as to the circumstances surrounding his unusual experience, and Mr. MICHALAK related the following story. He apparently had been prospecting approximately one mile West and two miles North of Falcon Beach. About 12:00 Noon he sighted the two space ships. He said they were rotating at a high rate of speed and emitted a red glow. The space ships landed near him and he reportedly touched one. The exhaust or some sort of hot substances

came off the space ship, burning his shirt, chest and hat. The space ships remained awhile, how long he was not certain, then flew away. He left the bush to get medical treatment.

4.   MICHALAK showed me his cap, the back of which was burnt. I wanted to examine his shirt, however, he would not let me, and kept backing away every time I got close to him. As far as I was able to determine, the back of MICHALAK's head was not burnt. It appeared to me that MICHALAK had taken a black substance, possibly wood ashes, and rubbed it on his chest. At no time during my conversations with MICHALAK would he allow me close enough to him to definitely see whether or not he was injured. I asked him why his hands were not burnt if he had touched the space ship and he would not answer me. At my request he drew a diagram of the space ship which appeared to be saucer shaped.

5.   I could not smell the odour of liquor on MICHALAK. His general appearance was not dissimilar to that of a person who has over indulged. His eyes were blood-shot and when questioned in detail could or would not answer coherently. I offered to drive him to Falcon Beach and arrange for some one to treat him but he declined saying he was alright.

6.   Approximately one half hour later, he came to the Detachment Office and asked for me. He would not enter the office, so I spoke to him outside. He wished to know where a Doctor could be located. I told him the nearest ones would be in Kenora, Ontario or Steinbach, Manitoba. He requested strongly that I not tell anyone what had happened to him as he did not want any publicity. MICHALAK said he was going to catch the 8:10 PM bus back to Win-

216

nipeg. He left and I later saw him sitting near the Falcon Beach Hotel on PTH#1, awaiting the bus.

7.   The information supplied by MICHALAK is of necessity vague due to his reluctance to co-operate. This reluctance of his part may have been intentional or due to circumstances beyond his control.

CONCLUDED HERE
(signature)
Cst. G.A. Solotki #23446. Falcon Beach Highway Patrol

APPENDIX B

Transcript of the recorded
interview conducted by
RCMP Corporal J. Davis with
Stefan Michalak on May 24, 1967

Corporal J. DAVIS, RCMP

This is an interview with Stefan MICHALAK, Taken at his residence at 314 Lindsay Street, Winnipeg, on May 24th, 1967, commencing at 1:45 p.m.

DAVIS: Steve, tell us what you did on Friday prior to the trip to Falcon Beach on Saturday.

MICHALAK: Well, in the morning I went to work at the Inland Cement Company and at 3:30 I punched out because I was already preparing myself from last year to continue my geological studies of the terrain. I am looking for special spots there which absorb my interest.

D: This is down in the Falcon Beach area?

M: Yes, it is.

D: What do you do with Inland Cement?

M: I'm working as industrial mechanic.

D: How long have you been with them Steve?

M: I've been with them for six or seven years.

D: Were you born in Canada?

M: No, I came to Canada in 1949 after discharging from the United States Army Occupation Troops.

D: Where were you born, Steve?

M: I was born in Poland.

D: You have been studying geology for some time, and prospecting as a sideline?

M: Yes, I went to Saskatchewan and to prospecting school at La Ronge and started a study on my own and I continue this. I like it, the land and the terrain and I continue it.

D: Okay, now you left work early on Friday afternoon

and the purpose was to catch the bus down to
Falcon Beach.

M: Yes.

D: And then tell me just what happened after you left
work on Friday, after you left your job at Inland
Cement.

M: Well, I came home to get ready, my wife made my
lunch, my son took me to the bus.

D: Did your wife make a lunch for you to use the next
day or for that night or for what?

M: Well, she made the lunch for the next day. There
was nothing to be spoiled.

D: What did she make for you?

M: I took some sausage and some cheese and some
apples, some buns, some oranges.

D: Did anything need any cooking at all that you
needed a fire for?

M: No. You see, I was going only for one day.

D: What other equipment, or what other articles did
you take besides your lunch?

M: I took with me besides the lunch, I take a magnet, I
take raw porcelain bricks for checking, an axe,
hammer.

D: What are they?

M: Raw porcelain, raw polished porcelain to check the
formation for streak and colour. I had this and I
took a magnet, compass, I took gloves, goggles,
hatchet, chipping hammer, books and my notes.

D: I see, the same stuff that any person prospecting
would take.

M: Yes, normal for simple prospecting checking.

D: And that's all, eh?

M: Yes.

D: And the clothing that you had with you?

M: And the clothing I had on.

D: Now, how did you get to the bus?

M: My son drove me to the bus, it was 7:15 I think from Winnipeg and I come about 9:30 – 10:00, 9:30 I think to Falcon Beach, something like that.

D: And then what did you do?

M: Then I checked into the room, I had room number 13 I think.

D: That's in the motel on the highway, eh?

M: Yes, that motel.

D: And what did you do after you checked in?

M: After I checked in, I studied my books for an hour, an hour and a half, then I went for coffee.

D: In the coffee shop in the motel.

M: In the motel, yes, and I talked to one gentleman for a little short time. I asked him if he has seen lately any geologists working around here. Well, he says they always do and it was very few words.

D: Was this man from the motel, do you know? Or was it a visitor?

M: Well, he was behind the counter so he must be the man from the motel.

D: I see, and then following that?

M: Following that I went to bed.

D: What time would you have gone to bed?

M: Well, I still checked my equipment that I have and then I went to bed.

D: Did you have anything to drink at all that night?

M: No, no I didn't.

D: No alcoholic beverages at all.

M: No.

D: All right. what time do you think it would be that you got to bed then?

M: I went to bed, it was about 10:30 something like that.

D: I see. Did you get up on your own the next morning or did they call you or what?

M: I get up on my own. It was exactly 5:30 when I got up.

D: And what did you do from that point?

M: I have a little lunch in the hotel room.

D: That you brought with you?

M: Yes, then I left the hotel. I left the key on the desk and I went to the bush.

D: Where did you go from the hotel? Did you walk up the highway or did you go straight in the bush?

M: No, I walk and the farthest I go is up to that booth where they are checking cars and then I turn north.

D: North off the highway?

M: Yes, off the highway.

D: All right, tell us just what happened. Nothing happened at all, I gather on the way in, eh?

M: Nothing happened. I checked a few quartz veins there which I spotted and do a little opening of moss and so on.

D: The area is familiar to you, Steve, you've been in there before?

M: I was last year in a little bit different place, same area, yes, the same general area. I was last year there.

D: But not since last year, is this your first time down there this year?

M: Yes, because the weather wasn't fit. The weather wasn't good at all so now the weather fit so I thought I would go and check. I am going to stick there. I can show my book, my geological book, the geology of Manitoba, exactly where I was going. This is one I took, I can show you for your own knowledge, where I am going.

D: Okay, fine. Now after you started in you kept going to the spot you had in mind, eh?

M: I didn't even waste time. I just reached the spot I
       was going.
D: You told me yesterday about running into a family
       of geese in there. Just what happened?
M: Well, when they see you first they start making
       noise. The female she starts making noise. Then the
       gander comes too, and they look at you. They are
       very suspicious and they look at you. But after they
       get quiet. I find some veins there, coarse veins and I
       start.
D: You were working quite close to where they were, eh?
M: Yes, well, I say 150 – 200 feet. There is a bank of
       rock, like a small ? and it was of my interest.
D: On your way in you would have been sort of
       working your way in, looking at rocks and so on
       along the way going in.
M: Yes, you do this because you contemplate on what
       you're looking for.
D: So you worked in the area where these geese were
       for awhile, eh?
M: Yes.
D: So what happened after that?
M: After that, the geese they quiet down. They get used
       to you. They always do. Well, then I start measuring
       the vein I found. I start stepping and counting my
       steps. I measure the width and the length as much
       as possible I can see. I open with my chipping
       hammer. Then at 11:00 o'clock, I look at my clock,
       and I have lunch. After lunch I go again on my
       work. The geese they are making noise then. They
       were running around on top the water, I see the
       mother goose was making a tremendous noise there.
       I was bending or kneeling over the ground, I lift my
       head and I look down to the swamp where the geese

were and it hits me that a light was coming from over there.

D: In the sky.

M: Yes, but at the moment I spot one, another one was following after the other, there were two. The shape is like the sketch I made, they fit in position and the colours, the blue sky and the mix with red. So they whirl around and quit.

D: Shut down?

M: It didn't make any noise at all.

D: While it was travelling through the air it didn't make any noise at all?

M: No noise at all. It landed and the other one stays about 10 to 12 feet above the ground.

D: Was it making a noise?

M: No noise at all.

D: What direction did these things come from?

M: They come from exactly, I'm positive, 255 degrees south, southwest.

D: To where you were standing?

M: That's right. So I took my map, the moment it took off, the last one, the moment the last one took off, so I see that it went in the same direction that it came from. So I set right away the map, I look into the map, I set the compass onto the map and I took the correct reading.

D: And it was 255 degrees.

M: Declination.

D: Declination, I see. Okay, what was the weather like Steve, at the time.

M: The sky was partially cloudy.

D: How high would the clouds be?

M: The clouds were pretty high.

D: A few thousand feet anyway?

M: Yes, a few thousand feet. Its hard to say.

D: What would you say your visibility was? Good?

M: Oh, visibility was good.

D: You could see a long way.

M: Oh yes, you could see a long way.

D: Was it windy?

M: No. Not much.

D: Was there any sign of any electrical storms in the area?

M: No.

D: Lightning or anything like that?

M: No.

D: Had it rained?

M: It rained about three or four hours after.

D: But before, no indication of rain at all, eh?

M: No, no rain at all.

D: Now what about your eyesight Steve?

M: My eyesight, its very good.

D: It's very good, eh? Do you wear glasses at all?

M: Do I wear glasses, I wear glasses for a close, particularly small job. I am wearing glasses at work.

D: When you're chipping at rock, you don't wear glasses for that, eh?

M: In that case I just use goggles.

D: These goggles you had on, what are they like? Could you describe them for me?

M: They are square type of goggles which fits over your prescription glasses. You can wear over prescription glasses. There is one clear lens and one number six colouring.

D: Number six colouring?

M: Yes.

D: When you were working when you first saw this light in the sky what lens were you looking through?

M: Through the clear glass.

D: And was the light quite bright?

M: Very bright.

D: Did you have to use the coloured glass to look at it?

M: No, it wasn't as much bright, but when it stops, the violet light which was coming from inside and blinking inside, I couldn't. I should say the light from inside was very light, almost white, white purple sharp just about like off hot water. It was hard on my eyes so I flip over the dark glasses.

D: All right, now getting back to these things approaching you from the south, southwest. What happened after you first saw them?

M: Well, I wasn't afraid, I know this, but it was a surprise, it catch you off for a moment, like you know, "Well, I'll be damned."

D: Yes, amazement.

M: Amazement, yes. I don't know for how long, but I think I never moved. I know that I didn't move. I was kneeling and I saw the thing and the other one took off. I know that my eyes were going from one to another. So after the other one took off I concentrated on this one.

D: They approached you and one of them landed, eh?

M: Yes, just one of them.

D: And how far away would it have landed?

M: It landed about 100, I can say about 100 feet.

D: What can... what kind of terrain did it land on?

M: Rock of the pre-cambrian shield.

D: Was there any nearby trees or grass or anything like that, or was it just bare rock?

M: No, it's bare rock, there was some little bush. It was kind of a clear spot. A little open place, yes. Naturally there's a little on the rock, old vegetation, leaves, you know, still wet.

D: What about the colour, the one that remained in the air, and hovered about 10 feet off the ground, what colour would it have been?

M: That one was the same colour, red, grey, red and then when it was vanishing it was turning slowly, orange, and then brighter orange and then grey orange as it was going in the distance, and turns grey and flicks one more orange and then disappears.

D: Was it revolving when it was hovering off the ground?

M: You can't see if it is revolving or not. You can feel probably by your inner feeling telling you that it is revolving but you can't see it. No you can't see it.

D: And the one that never did land it remained for how long, hovering above the ground?

M: That was, well it is hard to say, a short time anyway.

D: Would you estimate the time?

M: A short time, two or three minutes. That was the most.

D: And what did it do then?

M: It took off.

D: In what direction?

M: The same direction as it had come from originally.

D: Did it fly fast when it left?

M: Very fast.

D: Would you be able to estimate the speed?

M: Well, I have ideas of revolutions of motors but nothing travels so fast as this. We don't use our normal technology so fast as it was going.

D: The height and so on?

M: Yes, the length of this thing was about 35 – 40 feet in diameter from the centre edge to the edge.

D: And the height?

M: The height, I put three lines in making my sketch so I filled the straight lines only, like this one from this height was four feet approximately four feet and 2 to 3 so it was approximately 11 feet.

D: Altogether?

M: Altogether. With a dome on top.

D: Now after the machine settled down, what did it look like after it was sitting?

M: Well, when the machine sits you can see the contours all very clear because it is not rotating anymore and as I make the sketch here it looks like, what should I say, it looks like nothing.

D: When it first settled down on the ground it was a bright red, like hot metal and then it gradually turned what?

M: Yes. It gradually turned to the grey, steel grey, silverish colour.

D: Like metal cooling off?

M: Yes, right, metal colour. It hasn't got the breakdown of the blue colours like zinc or antimony or any other alloy. It is more of a brass yellow, pale brass yellow colour which is similar to the same as stainless steel and it was so smooth finish that it was amazing me.

D: I see. I... how long did it sit there before you approached it?

M: Well, much more than half an hour.

D: It was just the last few minutes that it was there that you approached it.

M: It was the last few minutes that I approached it and I started talking to it.

D: And it sat there altogether for what?

M: A good 45 minutes. It was a long 45 minutes.

D: How long did it sit on the ground before the hatch opened?

M: About 10, I can't say, oh, about 10 minutes.

D: Did you hear any noise from the machine as it was settling down onto the ground?

M: Yes, it was a whirling noise or running small motor or like fast running, whistling, whirling sound and then I feel a suction of air.

D: Like an air suction?

M: Air suction.

D: After it was on the ground?

M: Yes, after it was on the ground.

D: And what kind of noise did it make apart from the air suction? Could you hear any motors running from inside or anything like that?

M: No. I didn't hear nothing beside this.

D: And after the hatch opened?

M: The hatch opened I saw the light.

D: Describe this light for me.

M: The light was a column, bright light. It was so bright and was many, many violet colours, different shades involved in it where you see the streaks on it, lines on the beam and heart shaped, rounded corners you can see holes just like on a photo, reflected on the ground.

D: The bright violet light was patterned on the ground?

M: It looks to me like it was coming from the top about 45 degrees from underneath the top of that dome.

D: From what you saw from inside the machine what about the walls how thick would the walls be?

M: It was at least 18 – 20 to 22 inches thick with the ribs inside like at first you have the imagination of grate, of grates something like grates.

D: In the walls, the ribs in the walls?

M: Yes.

D: The walls were 20 to 22 inches thick you feel, eh?

M: Approximately, yes,

D: And then when you approached this machine, just what happened? You gradually approached it and you spoke, eh?

M: When I started going I hear a noise. There was positive human being talking in there.

D: Men talking?

M: Men.

D: But a language you couldn't understand?

M: No, no. But the first idea which ever comes to me was Americans. So I say well, if you are Yankee boys, you come out and don't be afraid. I say I don't sell your secret for a lousy green buck, if you need help just come out. Then the voice stopped. Completely.

D: How many voices, any idea?

M: Well, I think it was maybe two, three times exchanging short conversation. And that was it. They never say a word after.

D: And after you spoke to them in English what did you speak to them in?

M: Then I say in German and Italian.

D: What did you say in German?

M: In German I say, " Sprechen sie Deutsch?"

D: And in Italian?

M: (Said several words in Italian) Comprends en Francais? Non savais. Then I said (said several words in Polish and Ukrainian).

D: This is Polish and Ukrainian, eh?

M: That's Polish, Ukrainian and Russian.

D: How many different languages are you familiar with Steve?

M: Five, six. I can manage. I can get along.

D: And then after you spoke in these different languages, how long would it be before the hatch began to close?

M: The hatch closed quickly and that was the only time I saw it was closed, I didn't saw how it was opened.

D: How would you describe it closing?

M: The closing was one plate moving horizontally and another one horizontally in the other direction and the third one was pushed out.

D: To form the outer shell, is that right?

M: To form like this, yes that what it means.

D: And you weren't able to see a seam, it was a very well-fitting door when it closed?

M: I couldn't tell you. It was very well-fitted. I didn't pay attention at the moment because...

D: As you got near it you could feel the heat radiating from it?

M: Oh yes, the moment I was stepping in it was not only I could feel it I can see the heat. The blossom on the colours on that metal tells me that the thing was hot so then I feel any step I come closer I can feel hotter and hotter.

D: After the door closed, did you hear engines start or anything like that?

M: No, just start turning red and started rotating to the counter-clockwise and...

D: Started turning red before it started to rotate?

M: Increased the whirling and then when it blows I didn't hear nothing anymore.

D: The heat that you got burned with came out a grill work on the side, eh?

M: Yes, it was on the side.

D: Were you standing near this grill work?

M: It was about 6 to 10 feet away from the openings, maybe more from the hatch.

D: Oh, the grill work was? And how far would you be standing from the grill work on the side of the machine?

M: Oh, from that blower I say the length of my hand.

D: You reached out and touched right beside the grill work, eh?

M: Yes, that's right.

D: And as the machine started to leave the ground, this was when you got burned, was it?

M: That's right, that very moment.

D: And the blast of heat spun you around?

M: That very moment, and it got my shirt.

D: Yes.

M: So I ripped my shirt off, one and another one and then I turn my head it was gone already away. It was going.

D: At a fantastic speed again?

M: Oh yes. It was very, very high speed.

D: You've seen jet aircraft flying, would it be flying a lot faster than a jet aircraft?

M: Oh yes. Jet aircraft makes about 100 times more noise than this one.

D: And what about the speed?

M: And the speed, you can't compare. You can't compare the speed. You might say three times, maybe four times maybe five times faster than jet. It's pretty hard to say.

D: And the colour of it as it was leaving you?

M: The colour gradually was becoming to be a real red. Increasing systematically and the farther it was the thing start changing to more orange and then the orange start vanishing and then comes to the clouds. I think comes close to the clouds when I see the very, very little orange flicker and that's all I see.

D: Was it gone into the clouds, into the cloud layer?

M: Yes. It disappear. I couldn't see. Shortly after I remember I start thinking, I say if this thing is an aircraft then its going to fall to the pieces. And it wasn't maybe two three minutes that there was aircraft passing. There's quite a bit of traffic there. Above. Well, I don't know if any of them indicate something, maybe not.

D: I want to ask you about the power lines. There were power lines in the area.

M: There are power lines about 200 to 250 feet from the highway #1 north, north of highway.

D: And how far would you be from the power lines when you saw these things?

M: Well from the power lines I was approximately 2 miles. Approximately, not quite maybe. It's really hard to say.

D: You touched this machine with your gloved hand. It's the mate to this yellow plastic glove you have here, right?

M: Yes.

D: And did it melt the plastic on the glove?

M: Well, it didn't melt it completely, it starts, it starts melting but I know it was slippery right away. And so I take off my hand.

D: Tell me about how this thing left the ground, did it just lift straight off the ground or did it tip on one edge?

M: It tips a little bit because I know I was already half naked cause I made a turn. I don't know because I'm not a weak man either and when I got up that shirt was just ripped off completely. And it tips a little bit.

D: And it climbed at a bit of an angle?

M: A little bit on angle so I can't see the top about 1 foot or two its hard to say. A little, you know, silver from the top I say. And then, no more.

D: Did it climb at that angle for awhile?

M: It just kept the way it was standing. The way it was standing it just went up there. It tip little bit and up she goes.

D: After you tore your shirt off, your outer shirt, you left that on the ground there, it was pretty well burnt up, eh?

M: Oh yes, I didn't care at all for my top shirt because there was no fire on the forest, it was not dangerous. I didn't care.

D: And your undershirt, you took it off and put it out and took it back with you.

M: Well, I didn't intend but after I sore up then I pick it up. I just tramp it and leave it there. After I distinguish the fire I was for a little while cruising around, you know, walking around if I was toring my shirt off. I was thinking that some pieces going to fall on the sides, you know and even later I... so I wait and I look at that spot there around and I measured my steps approximate length you know that I imagine the lines are how I could see them and then I check around for fire.

D: You were worried about starting a bush fire.

M: I saw a bush fire in my life so I know what it's like.

D: Did you see any marks on the ground where the machine had set down at all?

M: Nothing except blown out vegetation and a type of circle about 10, oh, about 10 feet.

D: Is there anything else that you left at the spot there?

M: I forgot my measuring tape, I think it's 8 foot, about

6 feet or 8 feet, 6 feet I think.

D: What about a saw, you told me something about a saw.

M: That saw is not on the place but that saw I find before on the way in the bush.

D: Somebody had left the saw in the bush.

M: Yes. Somehow on the way, yes, in the bush. It is a two-way saw, on one side is a rip saw, a crosscut and on the other side it is a swede saw. It's kind of an old timer's, you know, a wooden handle and a straight blade. So that saw would be probably be there again. If I missed it, if I missed a degree or something we can...

D: How far away would the saw be from the spot?

M: That saw is about half way out.

D: I see, half way out to the highway.

M: Half way by the culvert, I put on the stone, on a rock there.

D: How long did you stay at the spot after the machine left?

M: After the machine I stay maybe at the most 10 minutes.

D: Then you started for the highway?

M: Then I started feeling bad so I vomit there.

D: You say you felt sick then, eh?

M: So I start heeling to the highway, I say it's the only chance I have.

D: Did you vomit there? You felt sick right there, eh?

M: Yes, yes.

D: And how long would it have taken you to get back out to the highway Steve?

M: Oh, it takes me, I don't know, I was going very fast, I was going faster than before.

D: Did you feel sick quite shortly after the machine left?

M: It didn't... yes, I feel a little bit. Not much but then it gradually started increasing and increasing. I start vomiting, whether there was any more in me to vomit. Before I reach the highway I stopped there, you know, I was vomiting for maybe two minutes and then I went out. I was empty. And the smell from inside my body was coming smell of burning, that smell of the motors, the wire, the cables, burning like a wire or electric motor when it burns, the smell.

D: This is the taste you had in your mouth?

M: The taste and the smell I had.

D: I see. How have you been feeling since this happened?

M: Since this happened I don't feel very good.

D: Have you not been able to eat anything much?

M: I didn't eat, I just try today. I call and doctor order I ate today. This is my first toast and glass of milk.

D: And has your head been aching?

M: Head is still aching.

D: Still aching a little bit?

M: Still have black out today.

D: You did, eh?

M: In the car.

D: How much weight have you lost?

M: I average losing about 5 pounds day. I lost fifteen pounds already.

D: This is the fourth day since you had this experience?

M: Yes.

D: Steve, I want to talk to you about this smell. Is there any smell in the area?

M: It smells like you enter a big, large room where there is nothing but electrical equipment running and you can feel it.

D: Yes, with all that electrical equipment running.

M: That's right.

D: Did this smell remain after the machine left, or would you know?

M: Well, I can't tell you. It still smell a little bit.

RECORDING ENDS

ACKNOWLEDGEMENTS

This book has been many years in development, from concept to its final production.

The authors would like to thank the following individuals who contributed or assisted directly or indirectly.

First and foremost, our original co-author, Stefan Michalak.

Hal Anderson
M.J. Banias
Curt Collins
Geoff Currier
Norm Davison
Geoff Dittman
Heidi Dittman
Karen Hall, McNally Robinson Booksellers
Steve Hladkyj
Devin Imrie
Eva Michalak
Kristi Nowicki
Chris Reid
Donna Rutkowski
Sybil Stokoloff
John Toews, McNally Robinson Booksellers
Peiqing Wang
Peter Warren

BIOGRAPHIES

Stan Michalak

Stan Michalak is presently in the last of three professions he has enjoyed over his lifetime. The first, the military, took him to postings overseas including a UN peacekeeping tour while in army green, then a stint in air force blue after receiving his officer's commission. His second career was with local media – first radio news at CKRC, then television news and current events programming at CKND. His third, and likely last, endeavour is graphic design. He pursued art as a teen under his father's guidance but did not return to it until 1990 when he purchased his first Mac. Trained in the traditional mediums, Stan has enjoyed combining his art skills and the digital platform working in the magazine and book industries. He has published numerous articles in national publications and has a book of fiction in the wings. His Winnipeg home sports his artwork (and some of his father's) on the walls. He is an avid big-game hunter, angler, passionate golfer, an obsessive scale modeller of aviation subjects and spent many years performing musical comedy theatre on stage (and can still croon a Sinatra tune).

BIOGRAPHIES

Chris Rutkowski

Chris Rutkowski is a Canadian science writer and educator. Since the mid-1970s, he's written about his investigations and research on UFOs, for which he is best known. However, he has been involved in many other writing and media projects for more than 30 years, including TV specials (*The Monster of Lake Manitoba*, 1996), planetarium shows (*Moonlight Serenade*, 1983, and *Amateur Nights*, 1989) and newspaper columns (*Strange Tales*, in the *Northern Times*, Thompson, Manitoba,1984 to 1985). He has nine published books on UFOs and related issues, a collection of short stories and has contributed to many other volumes, both fiction and non-fiction. His second book, *Unnatural History*, was a comprehensive and historical survey of many kinds of paranormal phenomena in Manitoba, including ghosts, UFOs, Sasquatch and lake monsters, and documented many of his own investigations. His recent works include *A World of UFOs* (2008), *I Saw It Too!* (2009) and *The Big Book of UFOs* (2010). He is on Twitter (@ufologyresearch) and blogs at: uforum.blogspot.com. In addition, he is a book reviewer for the *Winnipeg Free Press*, appears often on TV and radio, teaches courses on writing and is on the board of the Manitoba Writers' Guild.